The Complete
SOCCER
GOALKEEPER

Tim Mulqueen

with Mike Woitalla

Human Kinetics

Library of Congress Cataloging-in-Publication Data

Mulqueen, Tim.
 The complete soccer goalkeeper / Tim Mulqueen with Mike Woitalla.
  p. cm.
 Includes index.
 ISBN-13: 978-0-7360-8435-2 (soft cover)
 ISBN-10: 0-7360-8435-5 (soft cover)
 1. Soccer--Goalkeeping. I. Woitalla, Mike, 1964- II. Title.
 GV943.9.G62M85 2011
 796.334'26--dc22

                          2010040080

 ISBN-10: 0-7360-8435-5 (print)
 ISBN-13: 978-0-7360-8435-2 (print)

This publication is written and published to provide accurate and authoritative information relevant to the subject matter presented. It is published and sold with the understanding that the author and publisher are not engaged in rendering legal, medical, or other professional services by reason of their authorship or publication of this work. If medical or other expert assistance is required, the services of a competent professional person should be sought.

Acquisitions Editor: Tom Heine; **Developmental Editor:** Carla Zych; **Assistant Editors:** Michael Bishop and Elizabeth Evans; **Copyeditor:** Patrick Connolly; **Indexer:** Dan Connolly; **Graphic Designer:** Joe Buck; **Graphic Artist:** Kim McFarland; **Cover Designer:** Keith Blomberg; **Photographer (cover and interior):** John Dorton, unless otherwise noted; **Photo Asset Manager:** Jason Allen; **Visual Production Assistant:** Joyce Brumfield; **Photo Production Manager:** Jason Allen; **Art Manager:** Kelly Hendren; **Associate Art Manager:** Alan L. Wilborn; **Illustrator:** TwoJay!; **Printer:** Sheridan Books

Human Kinetics books are available at special discounts for bulk purchase. Special editions or book excerpts can also be created to specification. For details, contact the Special Sales Manager at Human Kinetics.

Printed in the United States of America   10   9   8   7   6   5   4   3   2

The paper in this book is certified under a sustainable forestry program.

Human Kinetics
Web site: www.HumanKinetics.com

United States: Human Kinetics
P.O. Box 5076
Champaign, IL 61825-5076
800-747-4457
e-mail: humank@hkusa.com

Canada: Human Kinetics
475 Devonshire Road Unit 100
Windsor, ON N8Y 2L5
800-465-7301 (in Canada only)
e-mail: info@hkcanada.com

Europe: Human Kinetics
107 Bradford Road
Stanningley
Leeds LS28 6AT, United Kingdom
+44 (0) 113 255 5665
e-mail: hk@hkeurope.com

Australia: Human Kinetics
57A Price Avenue
Lower Mitcham, South Australia 5062
08 8372 0999
e-mail: info@hkaustralia.com

New Zealand: Human Kinetics
P.O. Box 80
Torrens Park, South Australia 5062
0800 222 062
e-mail: info@hknewzealand.com

E4886

To my loving and supportive wife, Kathleen,
and to my beloved children, Trevor and Cate.
Thank you for helping me follow my dreams. I love you.

Contents

Foreword

I f you ask me when I really knew I wanted to be a goalkeeper, I trace it to when Tim Mulqueen started training me at a New Jersey soccer camp when I was 12 years old. He made me feel like I was doing something special.

Before that camp, I was a kid on the team with enough skill to score goals while on the field and prevent them when I took my turn in the goal. Then came the camp. Coach Mulqueen took aside the kids who volunteered for keeper training. That in itself was intriguing. We would be doing something unique, something the rest of the campers weren't doing. And Tim was enthusiastic in a way that made us feel like we were on a special mission.

When he trained us, I soon became aware that goalkeeping wasn't just about getting your body in front of the ball to block shots and catch balls. As Tim showed us the fundamental techniques and revealed that making a save required a precisely executed series of movements, the position took on a whole new meaning and became even more enjoyable.

Coach Mulqueen showed us how much skill and thought go into goalkeeping. Because of that, it became a fascinating challenge. I realized that there is an art to goalkeeping, and I was improving dramatically. It's a long road to mastering the position. But I was a better goalkeeper after each session with Coach Mulqueen.

After that first camp, I started going to Coach Mulqueen's weekly goalkeeper sessions and played for his club team. When I was selected to Olympic development program teams, there he was, ready to train the keepers. Amazingly, he would also coach me when I became a pro with Major League Soccer's Metro-Stars (now known as the New York Red Bulls) and on occasions with the U.S. national team.

Coach Mulqueen has coached keepers of all ages, from youngsters to seasoned pros. And it's remarkable how similar his methods are at each level. Of course, at the younger ages, the training isn't as vigorous. His demeanor adjusts accordingly to children, who need more patience and inspiration than pros. He knows when players are physically and mentally prepared to move on to new challenges. But goalkeeper fundamentals are the same for all ages.

Tim was more than a coach to me. He helped me mature both as a player and as a person. He showed me how to respect others and how to earn respect. He even nagged me about my studies. And now that I've spent years playing in the English Premier League, I see how his influence helped me attain that success—and how his approach provides an excellent example for other goalkeeper coaches.

So much about good goalkeeper training is the ability to teach proper technique and to run fun and productive practice sessions. But there's much more to it than setting up drills. Exceptional goalkeeper coaches build confidence, critique effectively, and help players learn how to read the game. That's why this book is more than a series of exercises: It delves into all the aspects of the position and the coach–player relationship.

However crucial good coaching is, the responsibility does ultimately rest on the player. And that's what makes this book so valuable to the future of goalkeepers— it speaks to both the player and the coach.

Tim Howard

Everton goalkeeper in English Premier League and U.S. National Team member

Preface

You've made a brave decision to become a goalkeeper or to coach a keeper. You don't have to be the best defender, the top midfielder, or the most prolific striker on the team to get on the field. But only one keeper gets the call. You can be the second-best goalkeeper in the league, but if you're not the top keeper on your team, you stay on the bench.

The goalkeeper is at times the most celebrated player on the field and at other times the loneliest. A series of spectacular saves is quickly forgotten when the ball hits the net behind the keeper. A field player can cough up the ball, misplay a pass, or botch a tackle, and usually the mistake will create no severe consequence. But a keeper errs, and his team gives up a goal, perhaps the championship.

But keepers win championships. We see it so often—the dominating team loses the game to the opponent with the better goalkeeper. Diving saves make the highlight reels. A keeper stops a penalty kick or stifles a breakaway, and the momentum swings his team's way. The glory of goalkeeping is the reward for the risk and the hard work required for excelling in the high-pressure position. A pat on the back from a coach, a high-five from a teammate, and the roar of the crowd after tipping away the shot that was headed into the upper corner make it all worthwhile.

In the optimal youth soccer environment, players are allowed to explore all the various positions on the field. Some will be drawn to the unique role of goalkeeper. When a young player falls in love with the position and is ready to accept the rigorous physical and mental demands, he'll train as no other player in soccer does.

Preparing to handle every possible goal-scoring opportunity not only means mastering the technique of shot stopping or cutting off the cross, but it also requires gaining the tactical acumen that enables the keeper to predict the unfolding of a foray. Reading the game, communicating with teammates, and organizing the defense are traits that come from proper training.

The keeper spends part of practice training individually to hone technical skills and to reach optimal fitness and agility. Then the keeper trains with the team, which depends on the keeper not only to lead from the back but to inspire confidence and give direction. So the keeper and coach have a relationship unlike that of the field players and coach.

Many teams, even at the youth level, have goalkeeper coaches charged with getting the best out of the players who take on this crucial role. When a keeper coach is not available, the head coach or assistant needs to know how to provide the unique training a goalie requires. This book adds to the repertoire of advanced goalkeeper coaches while offering tips and methods for coaches without goalkeeping backgrounds to ensure that they can meet the needs of their keepers at practice and at game time.

Goalkeeping requires a strong partnership between keeper and coach; that's why this book is directed at both individuals. The goalkeeper coach's role is that of trainer, teacher, critic, psychologist, and friend. Methods that inspire some keepers may not work with others, which is why we explore the myriad approaches that keepers and their coaches have embraced.

Many exercises are included in this book—not because you need to incorporate them all in one day or one week of practice! You will find that certain exercises will become staples of your practices, some will add variety to the usual routine, and some will be appropriate when particular areas need work. Other exercises build confidence and will become the go-to drills that get you ready for game time. This book will enlighten you on the many facets of goalkeeping and guide you continually on the quest to master the position. Whether you find yourself struggling to handle crosses or battling a dip in confidence, you can turn to this resource for exercises and advice.

The diagrams and photos make it easy to set up the exercises, which can be adapted to suit keepers' ages and skill levels. But there is much more to becoming a great keeper than doing drills. That's why it's so important to share the on-field and off-field experiences and perspectives of top-level players—from today's best American keepers to international heroes of the past.

I have coached keepers on youth recreation teams and travel teams and at the college level. I have enjoyed training some of the nation's top keepers at U17 and U20 world championships and at the Olympic Games. I have coached veterans in Major League Soccer with the aim of keeping them sharp year-round, and I have also trained keepers during the short period of preparation for major tournaments. I have seen excellent athletes whose competition results didn't match their actual physical talent because they didn't conquer the mental aspects of the position. I have seen keepers with athletic deficiencies who, thanks to their smarts and fortitude, have reached great heights.

Goalkeepers, regardless of inevitable setbacks, must quickly regain a sense of invincibility. Such confidence is created by the on-field and off-field preparation. Taking the right approach at the right time is a talent that both the coach and the keeper must master. My aim has been to get the best out of all the keepers whom I have spent hours with, but they have also taught me so very much. These lessons have made me better at training and guiding the next keeper, and they can help you become the best you can be, whether you are the coach or the keeper.

Acknowledgments

This book would not be possible without the help of Tim Howard, Jason Riley, John Dorton, Tom Heine, and Carla Zych.

I would also like to acknowledge the many players and coaches who have taught me so much about the game, especially my mentor, Bob Gansler.

Key to Diagrams

GK	Goalkeeper
S	Server
CO	Coach
X	Defending player
O	Attacking player
- - →	Path of ball
⟶	Path of player
•	Soccer ball
△	Cone

Metric Equivalencies

Throughout the text, distance measurements are given in yards. One yard is roughly equivalent to (slightly less than) one meter. Approximate equivalencies for distances regularly referred to within the text are provided here:

1 yd ~ 1 m

6 yd ~ 5.5 m

12 yd ~ 11 m

18 yd ~ 16.5 m

50 yd ~ 45 m

100 yd ~ 90 m

130 yd ~ 120 m

chapter 1

Is That a Keeper? Assessing and Selecting Goalkeepers

"Some people say goalkeepers are crazy, but to me they're not crazy, they're different"—this is how young Ronnie Blake put it in Brian Glanville's insightful novel *Goalkeepers Are Different* (London: Virgin, 1971). Ronnie was a 12-year-old winger when his team's goalkeeper got hurt in the middle of a game and Ronnie ended up between the posts. "Nothing happened for a while. . . . I just stood and shivered and felt sorry for myself, till suddenly the other side came away and there was this forward coming through on his own." Ronnie made the save and enjoyed the praise of teammates. He went on to make a couple more stops. "From that moment, I was a goalkeeper," says Ronnie.

Ronnie recalls that nobody proclaimed that he was a goalkeeper or even asked him about a position change. "They just naturally assumed it." They saw that Ronnie had the qualities it takes for the high-pressure job. And Ronnie thought they might be right. The forward whom Ronnie thwarted was a "pretty big bloke," but Ronnie hadn't been afraid. With that realization and with the thrill he felt when he was hugging the ball after his diving save, Ronnie was hooked.

Indeed, goalkeeping is infectious. And it attracts the most competitive of individuals. That's not to say that field players aren't highly competitive—of course they are. But a young player who is drawn to the keeper position will display a special kind of confidence.

Players who want to be keepers don't mind being different. In fact, they relish it. They think of themselves as unique. Sometimes they even consider themselves as being in an elite group. You'll notice this when you observe keepers with each other. They look out for each other. They understand that what they do is their thing—unlike what any of their other teammates do. And their position *is* unique, requiring its own uniform, a special set of rules that apply only to the goalkeepers, and a straightforward responsibility: Keep the ball out of the goal!

I've seen plenty of players like Ronnie—kids who catch the keeper bug. But how does a coach figure out whether a player actually has the potential to be a great keeper? It would be unreasonable to expect young boys or girls to resemble a polished, mature goalkeeper; however, they do reveal signs of their budding ability. Look for the youngster who makes an effort to get a hand or foot on even the unsavable shots. Notice how quickly the player moves to the ball. An observant coach who is familiar with all the key attributes of a great goalkeeper will be able to spot the players with the most potential.

COURAGE AND CONFIDENCE

Above all else, goalkeepers must be brave. They must be willing to put themselves in harm's way. They must be willing to slide at a forward's feet to snatch the ball away without fear of getting hurt. And if they show any hesitation in courage—if they shy away from confrontation or contact—they're not suited for the position of goalkeeper.

Goalkeeper is a very confrontational position. A keeper must be able to challenge the shooter. But keepers must also be able to take charge of their own team. They cannot hesitate to give direction to their defenders. Sometimes the keeper needs to move defenders to spots where she wants them even if they don't like it.

Courage, confidence, and assertiveness—without these qualities, even the players with the strongest athletic tools will not be successful in the position of goalkeeper.

NERVOUS NELLIES NEED NOT APPLY

To spot the players who have the psychological tools to play goalkeeper, a coach must closely observe them in practice and game situations and must study how they interact with teammates. Body language speaks volumes. Of course, you can't expect young goalkeepers not to show some signs of disappointment right after the ball hits the net, but you should keep your eye on them a little longer and read their expressions once the game has restarted. Are they focused and ready for the next challenge, scanning the field and positioning themselves? Or do they reveal anxiety about the next shot, remaining timidly glued to the line with a slumped posture and fear in their eyes? Good keepers can't wait for the next shot so they can prove themselves.

When players take a turn in the goal, notice what they say to their coaches and teammates before and after the experience. Do they focus on what the other players are thinking? Do they voice concerns about giving up goals? Do they indicate that they are worried about their performance? Worry cannot be in the goalkeeper's psyche. Watch and listen for evidence of inner stability as well as a calm outward demeanor.

A good sign is when a keeper is still eager to play the position after he's given up a goal, even if the ball went between the keeper's legs because he lost focus for a second. Goalkeepers must have the ability to bounce back from setbacks, and even young players who are new to the position can show signs of resilience. Does the keeper quickly grab the ball out of the net and throw it out for the kickoff, clapping his hands to signal to teammates that one goal doesn't mean a disaster? Or does the keeper mope and hide his face?

Players who aren't calm and self-reliant won't be able to handle the position. Nervous Nellies simply won't excel between the posts. For coaches, determining which players have the necessary fortitude is a matter of knowing your players. Indeed, coaching goalkeepers, as with coaching other positions, isn't just a matter of instructing and training; it's about recognizing players' strengths and weaknesses—and judging their potential.

WHEN THEY'RE YOUNG

For the young age groups, keepers should be rotated frequently. If your league uses quarters, it's easy to use four different keepers in a game. At the U10 and U12 levels, coaches shouldn't make a player stay at goalkeeper for more than a half. At the U14 level, goalkeepers are ready to go the distance if that's their desire. However, many talented keepers are also good field players, and giving them some time in the field will keep them happy, help them learn to read the game, and give the other keepers valuable experience.

Keeping a player in goal for long periods prevents her from being around the ball and getting the touches that a youngster needs in order to develop as a player. The keeper on a dominating team can get bored, and the keeper on a team that is conceding plenty of goals can get discouraged.

On some teams, it may be difficult to get kids to volunteer for the position of goalkeeper. What can you do to change this? Assure them that they should go out there and have fun—and not worry about giving up goals. To raise the confidence of players and to help encourage them to take stints in the goal, you should incorporate some throwing and catching games into the practice. This can be done by including a few minutes of throwing, catching, and moving to the ball in the warm-up. When players are paired up for passing and trapping, have them switch over to some catching and throwing for a few minutes.

Team handball is a great game for encouraging would-be keepers. For a few minutes off and on during small-sided games and scrimmages, switch from soccer to team handball—which is like basketball with soccer goals. The rules can vary. Players may be allowed three seconds and three steps whenever they get the ball. For older kids, the rule can be that if a player in possession is tagged, she must turn the ball over to the opponent.

Team handball is fun, and it helps youngsters gain confidence in catching and throwing. This game helps develop field players as well as goalkeepers. Team handball is great for introducing a passing game because it encourages players to become aware of their teammates' positioning and spacing as well as how to get open to receive passes.

THE SIZE FACTOR

In general, the U14 or U15 level is when coaches seriously evaluate whether a keeper has the tools to truly excel at the position. Of course, one of the main factors for high-level play is size. In the younger age groups, a lot of coaches will peg a smaller kid as a prime keeper candidate. At this age, smaller players are

TOO SHORT?

Common sense tells us that taller goalkeepers (if they have the agility to handle low balls and possess all the other crucial traits) have an advantage over shorter keepers. But that doesn't mean shorter keepers can't have great success. The 5-foot-10 Nick Rimando helped Real Salt Lake upset the Los Angeles Galaxy—the star-studded team with David Beckham and Landon Donovan—in the 2009 MLS Cup. In fact, he made key saves in the penalty-kick shootouts that decided both the final and Salt Lake's semifinal win over Chicago. Major League Soccer's 2008 Goalkeeper of the Year was the Chicago Fire's Jon Busch, who also stands 5-foot-10.

Rimando and Busch may not have the size, but they possess very good athleticism and are able to read the game in a way that puts them in position to make saves. They're very explosive, incredibly quick, and extremely intelligent. They know that they are not going to come out for certain balls in the air, so they organize their team to take that into consideration. Rimando and Busch are among the keepers who have gone on to achieve great success at the game's highest levels despite being below the average height for the position.

| Jon Busch | Kevin Hartman | Troy Perkins | Tim Howard | Brad Guzan |
| 5-10 | 6-1 | 6-2 | 6-3 | 6-4 |

Each of these goalkeepers won MLS Goalkeeper of the Year Awards.

| Val Henderson | Jenni Branam | Hope Solo | Caroline Jonsson | Karen Bardsley |
| 5-7 | 5-8 | 5-9 | 5-10 | 5-11 |

Each of these goalkeepers played in the inaugural season (2009) of the Women's Professional Soccer league.

often more coordinated because of their more well-proportioned stature. Taller players may struggle with coordination because of their growth rate.

The tall lanky kids who sometimes move awkwardly—those who have the right ideas but might not be able to execute them because they have not settled into their body yet—might be the ones with the best chance of becoming great keepers. The smaller kids can fly around a little and look the part, but unless they are late bloomers, their chances of going far in the position may be limited. Sooner or later their lack of size is going to be a disadvantage—at least at the highest level.

Coaches shouldn't be impatient with the bigger players who struggle with coordination when they're young. The bigger keepers often take more time to develop their skills, especially footwork skills and the ability to save low and hip-height balls. The taller children tend to require more coaching—which is why youth keeper coaches must be patient and diligent.

At the U14 or U15 level, you might see shorter players who are technically gifted; however, unless there's an indication that these players have lots of growing left to do (e.g., the players' parents are tall), they probably don't have a strong chance of being top-flight keepers. That's not to say that shorter keepers can't be good high school or even collegiate keepers, but unless they hit a growth spurt, they're *less likely* than taller players to enjoy success at the pro level. Coaches should give players of all sizes a chance to develop physically and athletically before ruling them out as potential keepers.

LEAPS AND BOUNDS: EXPLOSIVE POWER AND ATHLETICISM

One of the key attributes for goalkeepers is explosive power. Especially in the case of close-range shots, keepers must be able to spring toward the ball from a standing position—without the luxury of the extra step. The easiest and most common way to test explosive power is the vertical jump test. In this test, the player leaps from a stationary position and slaps her hand on the wall. Before the jump, the player stretches one hand as high as possible, and that spot is marked. After the jump, the distance between the prejump mark and the point reached on the jump is measured. (Chalk or water on the athlete's fingers will help mark the jump spot.)

But be wary of putting too much value into an isolated analysis. The assessment should be based on players' overall athleticism—including explosive power, fitness, agility, and speed—as well as soccer-specific abilities. Skills must be considered together when evaluating young goalkeepers.

Kids' vertical jumps will increase as they mature. It's the same with other facets of the game. For this reason, strength is not of great importance in evaluating the play of young keepers. Coaches often ask, "When am I going to get my goalkeepers to kick the ball farther?" Well, when the goalkeepers get older, they will kick the ball farther. As long as keepers use proper technique, they will get stronger in time.

So a test such as the vertical jump shouldn't be overemphasized. Putting kids in goal and having them do the required activities provide an overall demonstration of their athleticism as it pertains to the position. Additionally, exercises in which the keeper moves in a manner that mimics game play are good tests of potential goalkeeping ability. Instead of relying on a single test, use soccer-specific drills that reveal whether players are fit and agile and whether they have the coordination and speed to do the job. The following exercises are good examples of this type of drill. In these exercises, the keeper weaves in and out of cones between catches and must move up and down to get to the ball.

Movement Exercises

Weaving and Catching—Shuffle Step

A good catch starts with the feet. To put themselves in the best position to grab the ball, goalkeepers must use lightning-quick foot movements. This exercise keeps the goalkeeper dancing and can be used to assess and train catching, saving low balls, saving mid-range balls, and diving. Adjust the service to match the keeper's skill level.

Setup

Place three cones 1 yard apart in a straight line. At the end of the line, use two cones to form a goal 5 yards in width, centered on the line. A server stands 8 yards behind the cone goal.

Procedure

The goalkeeper shuffles through the first three cones while facing forward. After moving past the third cone, the goalkeeper sets up in the cone goal. The server hits a volley to the goal, and the goalkeeper makes the save.

Repetitions

Perform six to ten repetitions.

Variations

Change the service to a drop kick. After weaving through the cones, the goalkeeper saves the drop kick. Change the service to a ball hit off the ground. After weaving through the cones, the goalkeeper saves the ball hit off the ground.

Advanced Variation

Have the server send balls to the sides of the goal. After shuffling through the cones, the goalkeeper moves to the cone that marks the right side of the goal and saves a ball (volley, drop kick, or shot off the ground) sent to the right side. On the next pass, the goalkeeper goes to the left and stops a ball sent to that side.

To further challenge the keeper, the server can send the ball to the opposite cone so that the keeper must move across the width of the cones to save the ball.

Weaving and Catching—Side Step

Setup

Place three cones 1 yard apart in a straight line. At the end of the line, use two cones to form a goal 5 yards in width, centered on the line. A server stands 8 yards behind the cone goal.

Procedure

The goalkeeper sidesteps over the top of the three cones. The keeper saves a volley, drop kick, or ball hit off the ground from the server. The keeper then repeats the exercise, facing to the left.

Repetitions

Perform six to ten repetitions.

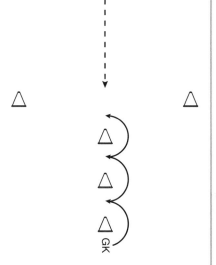

Down the Line, Up the Line

This exercise simulates the lateral movement that a keeper makes parallel to the goal line.

Setup

Place one cone in the center, a half yard behind what will be the goal line. Set up two goals, one on each side of and about 2 yards away from this center cone. For each goal, set up two cones 3 to 4 yards apart from each other. The servers stand in the middle of the two goals, 6 to 8 yards from the goals.

Procedure

The goalkeeper starts in the middle and moves down the line to his right. The keeper moves through the cone goal and saves a volley from the server. The keeper then moves back behind the line and behind the central cone. Next, the keeper moves down the line to his left. The keeper moves through the cone goal and saves a volley from the other server.

Repetitions

Perform six to ten repetitions.

Variation

Change the service to a drop kick or a service off the ground.

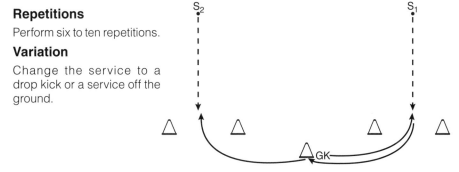

QUICK REACTION TIME AND A GOOD EYE

You'll hear people talk about goalkeepers making a reflex save. That's when the keeper—without having time to think—gets his hand, arm, fist, or foot in front of the ball fast enough to prevent a goal.

Sharp reflexes and quick reaction time are crucial attributes for a goalkeeper. Sharp reflexes enable goalkeepers to save close-range shots and to get their hands on balls that they see at the last second (e.g., when their view was blocked by other players). These are the saves that make the shooter wonder, *How'd he get a hand on that?* And if you asked the keeper, he probably wouldn't have an answer, because the save came thanks to lightning-quick reflexes. The moves that the keeper made to block the shot appear to be the product of an almost supernatural instinct.

Instinct and inherent ability aside, there are many ways to test and train reaction time and tracking ability. One method is to have keepers catch balls of various sizes. Start by tossing a golf ball to the keeper. Then throw a tennis ball, which will seem like a beach ball compared to the golf ball. When you follow up by throwing a soccer ball, the ball will seem enormous to the keeper. By throwing balls of any kind or size from close range, you can test and improve the goalkeepers' reaction time and focus. You can also incorporate different sized soccer balls. Start with a tennis ball, then move to a size 3 soccer ball before going to the size 5 ball. The players' eyes and hands have to work with different sized balls while the players' reaction time is being challenged.

A number of training exercises help develop reaction time as well as footwork. Almost any game played with a ball can be adapted for this purpose. For example, a coach or teammate can use tennis balls to play dodgeball with the keeper: The keeper stands in front of a fence or wall and tries to dodge balls thrown directly at him. The idea isn't to peg the keeper in the face, of course, but to give him a chance to work on seeing the ball and reacting to it quickly. The exercise that follows offers the same benefits.

Goalkeepers like exercises that involve the use of various kinds of balls because these exercises mix up the keepers' training routine while offering them a chance to hone their skills and work their fast-twitch muscle fibers (these muscle fibers generate short bursts of power and speed).

Reaction Exercises

Small Balls Against the Wall

Catching balls off a wall is excellent for improving a goalkeeper's reaction time, ballhandling, and footwork.

Setup

This exercise requires two golf balls, two tennis balls, a wall, and a coach or teammate to serve balls to the keeper. The keeper stands facing the wall, about 6 yards away from the wall. The coach or teammate (holding the golf balls) stands about 4 yards behind the keeper, also facing the wall.

Procedure

The server throws a golf ball against the wall, then immediately throws the second ball against the wall. The keeper should catch each ball without letting a ball bounce twice.

Repetitions

Repeat ten times with the golf balls, then repeat the set with tennis balls.

Variations

Have the keeper face the server. The keeper must turn quickly to snatch the ball as it comes off the wall. This variation simulates a game situation in which the keeper sees a shot late and must react quickly.

Tim Howard Turn

This exercise helps goalkeepers develop eye–hand coordination and body shape before the save. It's also a great technical exercise to work into the beginning of training.

Setup

Use a goal, or use cones to replicate a goal. If using an actual goal, place a cone in the middle of the goal to designate the area where the ball will be served.

Procedure

The goalkeeper starts at one of the posts (or cones), facing the corner flag. At the coach's command, the goalkeeper turns to save a service from the coach. The coach does not serve the ball until the keeper is properly positioned in the goal. After six to ten repetitions, the keeper changes sides and starts at the other post.

Repetitions

Perform six to ten repetitions on each side.

Variations

Vary the type of service.

FOOT SKILLS—IT STARTS EARLY

When goalkeepers reach their midteens and are serious about the position, they'll be competing for a starting spot on their club team. Some may be trying out for state or regional teams—or even the national team program. Goalkeepers who have mastered most aspects of the position may find themselves losing out to keepers who have better foot skills. Keepers with superior foot skills expand their team's options and opportunities in numerous ways.

Goalkeepers can't pick the ball up with their hands when it's passed back to them by a teammate; therefore, foot skills make all the difference.

TONY MEOLA'S METEORIC RISE

A good way to trace the rise of the U.S. men's national team is to track the career of goalkeeper Tony Meola. Meola grew up in the soccer hotbed of Kearny, New Jersey, and he proved that even very young keepers can attain international stardom.

In 1988, FIFA named the United States as the host of the 1994 World Cup, a decision that created a good amount of controversy because the U.S. national team had not qualified for a World Cup since 1950. If the U.S. team could not reach the 1990 World Cup in Italy, this would yield more criticism from the skeptics, who compared a World Cup being hosted by the United States to holding the baseball World Series in Brazil.

To qualify for Italia '90, the Americans would have to clinch one of the two spots from the CONCACAF region (North and Central America and the Caribbean). This feat was particularly challenging because the United States did not have a professional outdoor league; the North American Soccer League had folded in 1984. During the crucial phase of qualifying, Coach Bob Gansler gave 20-year-old Meola the starting goalkeeper spot.

At age 6, Meola was at first disappointed when his coach put him in goal. But Meola fell in love with the position because he got to dive around and go home dirtier than all the other players. Meola ended up excelling as a goalkeeper and a forward, in addition to starring in baseball.

Mark Newman was Meola's keeper coach at the University of Virginia, which won the NCAA title in 1989 with Meola in goal. Newman said that Meola ruled the penalty area, snatching crosses and intercepting through passes to eliminate the opponent's chances at goal before they became dangerous.

There was no doubt that Meola was the nation's best college goalkeeper after his freshman year at Virginia, but it was virtually unheard of to give a 20-year-old without professional experience the starting keeper position with a national team. Meola, however, proved that his excellent shot-stopping skills and his anticipation acumen translated to the highest level. He did not give up a single goal in the U.S. team's final four games of qualifying as the team booked its ticket to the World Cup in Italy.

The young Americans lost all three games at the 1990 World Cup, but Meola played brilliantly in a 1-0 loss to the host, and the team gained valuable experience. In 1993, Meola gave one of the greatest performances ever by a U.S. keeper in a stunning 2-0 upset over England. At the 1994 World Cup, Meola started all four games as the United States reached the second round, losing 1-0 to eventual champion Brazil.

By the time he retired, Meola had played in 100 games for the United States and had won college and MLS championships. He will forever be remembered for playing a crucial role in the rise of the U.S. national team, which has qualified for each of the last six World Cups, a feat matched by only five other nations.

Tony Meola played in two World Cups.

If keepers can confidently use their feet to deal with back passes, they give their defenders a valuable option when the defenders are under pressure. To do this, keepers must be able to settle the ball with either foot and pass the ball over various distances with precision. To illustrate how important foot skills have become, consider this: Goalkeepers touched the ball with their feet more times per game during the 2010 World Cup than during any previous World Cup, seven more times per game.

A keeper with limited foot skills will turn too many goal kicks and punts into 50-50 balls, meaning that the opponent has as much of a chance to get the ball as the keeper's teammate does. Goal kicks are often the first point of a team's attack, and having a field player rather than a keeper take a goal kick means giving up a numerical advantage in the field. Punting the ball isn't just a matter of blasting it upfield. The trajectory of the ball can give forwards an advantage. For example, a well-aimed low punt can find a wide player who has slipped away from her marker.

The goalkeepers who exhibit exceptional foot skills at the college level and beyond are most likely the ones who didn't specialize in the position too early. In fact, some of the greatest goalkeepers played in the field as well as in goal throughout their youth careers.

U.S. national team goalkeepers Tony Meola and Tim Howard were both center forwards in high school. That experience helped them in their ability to read the game and to use their feet. Meola's feet in goal were those of a field player. He was proficient with both his right and left foot, and his skill with his feet played a key role in how his teams played the ball out of the back.

Hope Solo, who won the Olympic gold medal with the U.S. women's soccer team in 2008, scored 109 goals as a forward in high school. She was a Parade All-American selection twice as a field player. Brad Guzan was a consistent starter in MLS at a younger age than any previous keeper (before he moved to the English Premier League). He played in the field for his youth club, the Chicago Magic, and for Providence Catholic High School, where he earned all-state honors as a midfielder.

These examples illustrate why it's important for young players and their coaches to realize that having the desire and the key attributes to be a goalkeeper does not mean it's time to specialize. Young players should take every opportunity available to develop their skills in the goal and out on the field. The following series of exercises is an example of the kind of activities that will help players hone their foot skills.

Footwork Exercises

Lateral Footwork: Shuffle

This exercise tests and improves the footwork that goes into preparing for the save.

Setup

Place three cones 1 yard apart in a straight horizontal line. Place a flag at each end of the line to form two goals; each flag should be placed 5 yards away from the end cone so that each goal is 5 yards in width. The keeper begins at the goal at one end of the line. A server stands about 6 yards from the cone at the end opposite the keeper.

Procedure

The keeper performs shuffle steps while slaloming through the cones. On reaching the goal at the opposite end of the line from where he started, the keeper receives a service and sends the ball back to the server. The keeper jogs back to the other goal and then repeats the shuffle through the cones. The server and keeper then reverse sides, and the keeper shuffles in the opposite direction.

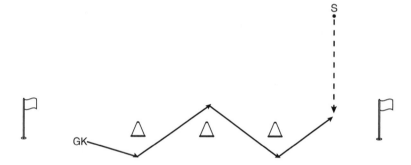

Repetitions

Perform six repetitions in each direction, with various types of service.

Variations

Place a server at each end or place the lone server in the middle to serve balls to both ends. The keeper moves from one end to the other and back three to five times.

Off the Post I

Setup

Set up three cones off both posts diagonally, forming a goal in the middle. The server stands about 6 to 8 yards from the goal line.

Procedure

The goalkeeper starts at the post, facing out to the field. The keeper steps over the top of the cones and saves a service from the middle. Next, the keeper goes to the opposite post and performs the same action over the cones. The keeper then saves another service from the middle.

Repetitions

Perform six to ten repetitions.

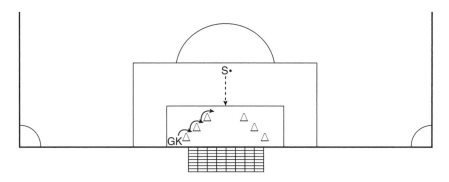

Variations

Change the service to a drop kick or a shot off the ground. Use this drill to work on low balls and mid-range balls. Have multiple servers in the middle.

MARY HARVEY:
THE FIRST U.S. WORLD CHAMP

The United States has produced many world-class goalkeepers. However, the first to win a world championship was Mary Harvey, a Northern California product who made several key saves for the U.S. team that won the inaugural Women's World Cup in China in 1991.

Not only did Harvey win a world title, but she was also the first U.S. woman to excel in a foreign league. After she starred at the University of California and graduated in 1986, Harvey figured out how to launch a career in the business world while sharpening her soccer skills.

She got a job with the management consulting firm Andersen Consulting, which stationed her in Germany, where the sports club system included highly competitive women's soccer. Harvey earned the starting keeper spot with FSV Frankfurt in the Frauen-Bundesliga. In 1990, she lifted the German Cup in front of 70,000 fans at the Berlin Olympic Stadium.

Harvey commuted across the Atlantic for U.S. national team duty. She was a team leader at the tournament in China that hailed the arrival of women's soccer on the global stage—while the United States set the standard.

Besides being a bold keeper who dominated the penalty area and possessed the lightning reflexes to make the close-range saves, Harvey excelled because she studied the game. She watched men's and women's soccer and learned how to anticipate the play. "She was very cerebral," said Anson Dorrance, the U.S. coach.

Harvey, who was Briana Scurry's backup when the U.S. team won the first women's Olympic soccer tournament in 1996, became the chief operating officer of Women's Professional Soccer when it launched in 2009. She credits her playing career for the success she's had off the field. This off-the-field success included an influential position with FIFA (soccer's world governing body) before she took charge of WPS.

"It absolutely fundamentally shaped the person I am today," she said to us. "It shaped me in business. It shaped me as a person. You learn you gotta take care of each other. It [the team mentality] becomes second nature, makes you a better person, and I'm pretty convinced I'm a better leader in my career [because of it]."

READING THE GAME: LEARN BY PLAYING

Field play does more than improve keepers' foot skills. It also improves their ability to read the game, understand and organize the defense, and anticipate an opponent's attack. By taking part in an attack, the keeper learns to comprehend how the attack unfolds. This knowledge enables keepers to intercept through balls—the passes that penetrate the defensive line to give an opponent a clear path to the goal—and to recognize danger spots when the opponent prepares for a cross.

Keepers must possess game intelligence. Game intelligence allows keepers to anticipate the play so that they can make the proper decisions, and it enables them to communicate to teammates where they need to move and where the keeper needs help. The best place for players to acquire game intelligence is out on the field. The need for goalkeepers to truly understand all aspects of the game is why we say a goalkeeper is just a soccer player who can use hands.

And, as unique as the position is, goalkeepers depend on their teammates just as field players depend on their keepers. Keepers who play other positions get a good appreciation for what a field player has to do. Have you ever heard a goalkeeper screaming at a player to get back and play defense after the player just made an 80-yard run? If you've ever made an 80-yard run, you know that it's not easy to get back right away and that being berated by your keeper does not help.

Despite the success that many U.S. keepers have had, some of the young keepers we see climbing to the elite ranks need improvement in the areas of foot skills, reading the game, and communicating smartly with their teammates. Many young keepers are excellent athletes who go far simply on their ability to make the emergency saves.

Making spectacular saves can indeed separate the great keepers from the good ones. But preventing a situation that requires the emergency save is the mark of the very best keepers; therefore, young keepers should constantly strive to improve in this area. There is only so much that a coach can do to help keepers "feel" the game. To a great extent, players must find it for themselves. That's why keepers should not specialize too early and should continue to get plenty of field time in their youth play.

Being a good field player can also create a more enjoyable soccer experience for young keepers. Beyond the variety and additional challenges, it can lead to more playing time. Each team only needs one goalkeeper at a time. A good field player can get action when it's another keeper's turn between the posts. Keepers who can play well in the field also get the extra respect of teammates.

CROSS TRAINING: OTHER SPORTS

The recent trend in U.S. youth soccer has been to discourage young players from participating in other sports. A lot of coaches worry that a player is going to fall behind if she doesn't play soccer—and goalkeeper in particular—all the time. I don't agree with that. Young people need to have a healthy balance.

If children and teens play soccer exclusively year-round, they can obviously suffer from burnout. In addition, the skills used in soccer correlate to those

SPOTTING POTENTIAL IN THE YOUNG GOALKEEPER

When I first saw Tim Howard at a camp I coached in Metuchen, N.J., he was 12 years old. I may not have said to myself, "Here's a kid who will play in the English Premier League." But I really did see the potential for greatness.

Very few goalkeepers will stand out as Tim did at such a young age. He displayed good footwork even before he began regularly doing goalkeeper-specific training. Players that young have much learning to do and will mature physically and mentally in many ways.

Already a big kid with exceptional athleticism, he displayed a healthy level of competitiveness. How does a coach measure competitiveness? Not by whether the player curses or gets upset after giving up a goal. A sure sign is when the kid tries as hard to make the save in the final repetitions of a rigorous drill as he does during a scrimmage.

Even at that young age, Tim always had the drive to succeed. He didn't just go through the motions during the more repetitive and less glamorous aspects of training. After the first camp Tim attended, he started coming to my weekly goalkeeper training sessions. He was always ready to give his best, always eager to get better.

I also immediately noticed that Tim showed respect for the other players and for the coaches. No matter how competitive or athletic a player is, a goalkeeper must learn proper technique. And that requires listening to coaches and taking advice.

Perhaps most importantly, it was obvious that Tim loved soccer and he loved playing goalkeeper. He continued playing in the field in high school, which is one reason why he reads the game so well, but from the first time I saw him it was clear that he embraced the goalkeeper position.

The key to spotting potential in young keepers is to look for their strengths. When I look at boys or girls playing the position, I don't pick them apart, detailing all their flaws to myself. I focus on what they bring to the table. I assess what they do well and consider how to build on that. And I ask myself some key questions:

Do they enjoy playing the position?

Are they brave enough for it?

Do they have the athleticism goalkeeping requires?

Are they coachable?

Being "coachable" means being eager to learn, ready to listen, and willing to work hard. No other position in soccer demands as much one-on-one time with a coach as goalkeeping does. Those youngsters who relish the intense training are those with the best shot at greatness.

used in basketball, baseball, or lacrosse. Therefore, playing other sports helps youngsters develop skills that translate over to soccer, and it also keeps the youngsters fresh. It's a win–win situation.

For instance, my son likes playing soccer—playing in the field and in goal—but he also plays basketball and flag football. I couldn't be happier, because when he goes to soccer practice, he wants to be there, he wants to play, and he enjoys it. If he did the same thing over and over, it might lessen his enthusiasm. Plus, he meets new kids. He gets into different social situations, which is an important part of life.

Brad Friedel and Tim Howard starred in both soccer and basketball in high school. Tony Meola kept playing baseball even at the University of Virginia while he was starring in goal and launching a national team career. Hope Solo played basketball and volleyball—*and* ran track. She says that if she played the same sport the entire year she would have gotten burned out. Instead, she says, the other sports helped her with agility, eye–hand coordination, and jumping ability.

Far earlier than previous generations, young athletes are being asked to focus on one sport and are being discouraged from exploring others. This early specialization has become one of the most controversial issues in youth sport—and not just in soccer. In addition to the psychological, social, and sport concerns associated with early specialization, studies have shown that it could be the reason for an increase in overuse injuries among children.

Regarding the increase in overuse injuries, Dr. Dev K. Mishra, an orthopedic surgeon and a member of the team physician pool with the U.S. Soccer Federation, wrote in the article "How much soccer is too much soccer?" in *Soccer America* "Many theories abound but most experts point to one main causative factor: year-round training in a single sport. What we are talking about here is structured, organized training. I cannot recall seeing these injuries in kids playing pickup soccer, hanging out at the park, or even playing several 'seasonal' sports."

Many goalkeepers love soccer and have a passion for the position. But that doesn't mean they shouldn't enjoy other sports. A varied experience enhances players' athleticism, which will help them when they eventually specialize.

Table 1.1 summarizes the characteristics goalkeepers should possess.

Table 1.1 Keeper Qualities

Psychological requirements
• Willingness to play in goal
• Competitiveness
• Self-confidence
• Bravery
• Unflappability
Physical requirements
• Explosive power and jumping ability
• Athleticism, including
• anaerobic fitness
• agility
• balance and coordination
• speed
• flexibility
• strength

Table 1.1

Technical requirements
• Body shape (GK ready position)
• Basic footwork: being ready for the shot while moving
• laterally
• backward
• forward
• Catching aptitude
• diving
• crosses
• shot stopping
• parrying
• Basic techniques with the feet
• trapping
• passing
• Falling for low balls
• Quick reactions
• Eye–hand coordination
• Breakaway response
• effective play
• use of techniques that help prevent injury
• Distribution skills
• throwing
• kicking
Tactical requirements
• Appropriate angle play
• Solid decision making on coming off the line
• Game-reading ability
• Organization of team
• defensive setup
• set plays
• counterattacks
• Smart distribution choices

chapter 2

Hero to Zero to Hero: Goalkeeping's Mental Challenges

Early in his career, English keeper David James allowed enough so-called soft goals that the British media nicknamed him "Calamity James." How did James respond? He set the all-time record for most games played in the English Premier League (more than 500), represented his national team more than 50 times, and was still going strong at the top tier at age 40.

All goalkeepers give up goals that they should have saved. What really matters is how they react after giving up a goal. The exceptional keepers learn from their mistakes, move on, and are confident that they'll keep improving. During the game, goalkeepers must always focus on the next play. Whether they give up the worst goal or make the best save, they need to get it out of their system and move on to the next play. In soccer, the next play is always the most important.

The mental approach that a player takes to the position will go a long way in determining how successful the keeper will be. Great talents have failed because of their mental approach. Less athletic keepers have thrived because of their smarts and fortitude. And it's not just about shaking off a setback.

The great German goalkeeper Sepp Maier said that the goalkeeper position, although it doesn't require running the distances required of field players, is just as demanding because of the intense concentration it requires. "Standing in goal for 90 minutes like a cat ready to pounce requires lots of energy," he noted in his book *Meine Towart Schule* (Germany: Heyne, 1978). For long periods of the game, goalkeepers will not get a touch on the ball, and then suddenly they have to make a play. They have a lot of time to think when the ball is on the other end, and their mental state when they're not near the action affects how they'll react when they are called on.

But staying focused during the lulls is just one of the challenges that the goalkeepers face. When they are under pressure—as the other team attacks—

goalkeepers need to be ready but composed. They need to remain calm in the midst of chaos, but they must be prepared to engage fearlessly when it's their time for action.

Goalkeepers who master the position are the ones who conquer the psychological demands. They have the character to rebound from a blunder in front of a full stadium. They have the patience to go most of the game without a challenge and then meet the challenge when it comes. Different goalkeepers will approach the mental challenges in different ways. But keepers can employ certain strategies that will help them play their best. And coaches can use certain training techniques and approaches to help keepers cope with the psychological demands of the position.

READING THE BALL—LITERALLY

One of the most common blunders occurs when the goalkeeper takes his eye off the ball before he has it under control. Instead of catching the ball, he lets it slip past him into the net or gives up a rebound that offers the opponent an easy scoring chance. Even great keepers make this mistake. Manchester United's Edwin van der Sar, for example, set an English Premier League record by not conceding a goal in 1,311 minutes. Then he bobbled an unthreatening long-range shot by Newcastle's Jonas Gutierrez, allowing an easy tap-in on the rebound.

These lapses occur when goalkeepers watch the ball until it's *almost* in their hands—they take their eye off the ball too early because (a) they're thinking about their next move or (b) they have deemed the shot tame, which causes them to relax and lose focus. One way I teach young keepers to concentrate is to have them read the ball, literally. For young players, I'll write numbers on the panels of the ball. When the players catch the ball, they read aloud the number in the panel facing them. This encourages them to focus solely on the ball and not on anything external.

I got the idea from a baseball anecdote about the great Ted Williams. To show his concentration and ability to follow the ball all the way to the bat, he put shoe polish on his bat. When he hit the ball, he would announce, for example, "over the left seam." The story goes that his teammates would look at the ball after it had been hit, and sure enough, the ball would be scuffed over the left seam. I applied the concept behind this anecdote to goalkeeping.

With older keepers, I have them read the script on the ball. They catch the ball and announce, "Inflate to 7 to 9 pounds" or "Made in Pakistan." When they're asked to do that, they get used to keeping their eyes on the ball until it's firmly in their hands.

STAYING SHARP

Shortly after he moved from Major League Soccer to Manchester United (the top team in the English Premier League), Tim Howard said that the most difficult thing he had to learn was to cope with the long breaks in the action. With the MetroStars, Howard got a lot of work. But Manchester United dominated most of its opponents, and action in front of the team's own goal could be rare.

ARE GOALKEEPERS CRAZY?

Goalkeepers have provided the world of soccer with many of its most colorful characters, creating the notion that playing the position requires craziness. In South America, the most common nickname for goalkeepers is "El Loco"—the crazy one. The theory goes that the truly sane couldn't handle the pressure.

Shep Messing, who played with Pele on the New York Cosmos, became one of the first U.S. goalkeeper stars. In *The Education of a Soccer Player* by Shep Messing and David Hirshey, he said that his conversion from forward to keeper came when he realized the following: "I was made for the position, a little crazy and a little hooked on body contact" : (New York: Dodd, Mead & Company, 1978).

Tino Lettieri, an Italian-born Canadian who starred in the North America Soccer League in the late 1970s and 1980s, kept a stuffed parrot named Ozzie in the back of his net. Lettieri would consult the parrot before penalty kicks for advice on which way to dive.

German keeper Sepp Maier, considered one of the world's best in the 1970s, often appeared in public wearing goofy costumes. Just minutes before a European Cup final, he joked around with fans; then he went out and helped Bayern Munich win the game. In one of his most famous incidents, Maier chased a duck that had strayed onto the Munich Olympic Stadium field while his team was at the other end. Maier dived at the duck, intentionally missing a capture each time as the crowd roared with delight.

Mexican goalkeeper Jorge Campos, who often wandered far out of the penalty area and juked his way past opponents, wore garishly colorful uniforms—including bright pink—and starred in two World Cups.

But of course there are many more goalkeepers who go about doing their job quietly and effectively. Maier himself said the position doesn't require one to be crazy. More important is passion, as he notes in *Save!* by Mark A. Newman, "I loved to play. I love to be goalkeeper." (Virginia: Mind's Eye Press, 1993).

Howard went through stretches without seeing the ball and then was called on to be sharp. That may be the most difficult part of goalkeeping: You're not involved in the action for a long period, and then suddenly you have to make a save.

The best way to stay on top of the game is by playing along in your head. Move with the ball, even though it's at the other side, so you stay loose and limber and feel as if you're a part of the game. Then you have to concentrate and remind yourself that at any moment something could happen. Tell yourself the following: *I could be called on to catch a cross, I might have to make a save, and at any moment I may have to come out and clear the ball with my feet.* Having these conversations with yourself will help you stay sharp. If you don't have them, then you're likely to experience breaks in your concentration and dips in your anticipation. And when you're called on to act, you'll react slowly.

Younger keepers in particular may have a difficult time keeping their focus. Coaches need to instill in young keepers the habit of keeping close track of the game so that the keepers can anticipate shots. One method of doing this is to have the keepers call out names in practice. For example, during a small-sided game, have the keeper call out the name of the player who shot the ball—the keeper must recognize who is shooting and from where. Especially during a tight game, the keeper can use this strategy to stay in tune with what's going on.

ORGANIZATION AND LEADERSHIP

Goalkeepers who do a good job of organizing their team—moving players around in specific areas—are helping their teammates prepare for an opponent's attack while keeping themselves alert. But we're talking about useful instructions, not cheerleading.

Shouts such as "Let's get the ball" or "Let's work hard" are nonsense. The instructions need to be specific, such as "Kyle, watch number 10!" Effective communication from the keeper may involve telling outside players to tuck in, making sure all the attacking players are defended, or giving defenders positioning advice—for example, "Move wide, Sally! Move wide! Number 2 is overlapping!" Using specific names and numbers keeps the goalkeeper in tune with what's going on so her mind doesn't drift or wander.

Such organizing takes place even when the keeper's team has the ball. The keeper continues to communicate with the players closest to her. We call this situation "resting defense." You want to be prepared in case the ball turns over. The keeper must anticipate where trouble could come from and must ensure that there are enough players in that area to prevent or quickly shut down a threat. The keeper's instructions help defenders stay ready to work as a coordinated unit the instant a counterattack is launched.

It's the goalkeeper's responsibility to monitor and direct the play. Because the keeper is not directly involved in the action, she can see what's going on and can provide some clarity on where things could develop. The keeper is not off duty just because the opponent isn't threatening. But when the pressure is on and the field players are losing their heads, that's when the keeper's leadership is most important. The goalkeeper needs to be a calming influence and needs to be clean and technically sharp. In this situation, a keeper can either add to the chaos or help her team get back on track.

An uptight keeper won't help frazzled defenders regain their composure. A misplayed ball that leads to a score won't lift their spirits. But a calm, confident keeper who handles the ball cleanly can rally her team and put the brakes on the opponent's momentum. This keeper can put a rebound into a safe area or hold a shot to buy time for her team to regain its composure, regroup, and reorganize.

Staying cool amid chaos comes from good training. I tell my keepers the following: "Everything you'll see in the game, we've trained. So nothing will be a surprise." It's like taking a test at school. If you've studied and are prepared, there's no cause for anxiety. Through her attitude and actions, the keeper should relay that sense of preparedness and confidence to her teammates.

MUTUAL RESPECT

The keeper who treats his teammates well is more likely to effectively motivate his team and more likely to be treated well in return when he needs a confidence boost. One mistake that keepers make is communicating in counterproductive ways during a game. They may do this by being too harsh on their defenders or by complaining when they shouldn't.

BRIANA SCURRY: POISE WINS

Brandi Chastain's clinching penalty kick—and her jersey-shedding celebration—may be the most famous image from the U.S. team's victory in the 1999 Women's World Cup (a victory that took place in front of a Rose Bowl crowd of 90,000 and a U.S. TV audience of 40 million). But Chastain could seal the victory only because Briana Scurry saved the shot from the spot by China's Liu Ying.

Scurry conceded only three goals and recorded four shutouts on the U.S. team's path to the title at the 1999 World Cup. In 1996, Scurry, a Minnesota product who starred at the University of Massachusetts, helped the United States win the first inaugural women's Olympic tournament.

But Scurry lost her spot in goal for the 2000 Olympics because she didn't keep herself as physically fit as a top-level keeper needs to be (and she suffered injuries as a result). When she watched the U.S. team lose the gold-medal game in Australia, she became determined to come back stronger than ever. She ate better and trained harder. "My goal was to be the fittest player on the team, not just the fittest goalkeeper," she said in *U.S. Soccer Communications,* February 26, 2003. After a nearly two-year absence from national team play, Scurry won back her starting position and helped the United States win the gold medal in 2004.

In total, Scurry played a record 167 games for the national team and established herself as the best women's goalkeeper of her era. Tony DiCicco, the goalkeeper coach who was head coach during the 1999 World Cup win, said that besides Scurry's knack for making the extraordinary save, she had the ability to actually become calmer as the tension of a game increased. He also said that Scurry's poise translated to her teammates.

Briana Scurry makes a save in the 1999 Women's World Cup.

© AP Photo/Paul Sakuma

Some keepers, for example, will make a save and then get up and bark at their teammates for allowing the shot. Many of today's young goalkeepers get agitated when they make a save. Here's what I tell the goalkeepers: "That is your job! That's why you're back there—to make saves and to help your team. Remind yourself that it's part of the job description: You're going to have to make saves!"

Many shots are taken simply because of good attacking play. But even when a teammate errs, there's no need to verbally cane that teammate. It's one thing to help teammates stay alert, but it's another thing to scold them and add insult to injury.

If the keeper treats his players with respect, then the keeper is likely to get support when he needs a lift. Teammates want to play hard for that kind of goalkeeper because they think, *Hey, he's picked me up. He didn't embarrass me in front of all these people. So now when I can do something for him, I'm going to lay out and do it.* It's a reciprocal effect. And the whole team benefits.

When a goalkeeper is struggling with confidence (perhaps because of a disappointing outing in the last game), it may be useful for the coach to speak with his teammates, especially the backs. They need to know what frame of mind the keeper is in. The coach can explain to the defenders that the keeper is going through a rough patch. Encourage them to get the keeper involved in the game early by using a safe back pass. Tell them that if the keeper does something well, they should give him a shout, such as "Good job!"

DEALING WITH SETBACKS

All goalkeepers will make their share of mistakes. It goes with the territory. And goalkeeper is a position where errors are amplified. Soccer is a low-scoring game. When a keeper blunders, the mistake will be highlighted. When a pro lets a ball slip between his legs or misjudges a cross that leads to a goal, the play will be shown over and over in the highlight reels. It may even become a YouTube hit. Rather than be paralyzed by embarrassment and frustration, though, keepers can take steps to regain their composure and effectiveness—and the keeper coach can help.

They Scored—Now What?

Goalkeepers react in various ways after they get scored on. Some keepers whack the ball in anger. Some fall to their knees, head in hands. Some scream at their teammates. And some hang forlornly on the net. Whether the keepers realize it or not, these immediate, emotional responses are more than personal reactions. These actions speak loudly to the keepers' own teammates and to their opponents.

So what's the best way to react? Keep your composure. Your teammates don't want to see you falling apart as if you've lost all confidence. They certainly don't want to be berated. If they were at fault, they most likely already know it. If they weren't, they'll resent being blamed. If something needs to be discussed, it should be discussed concisely and without drama.

What should you do with the ball in the net behind you? Don't embark on a long sprint, carrying the ball to midfield to speed up the kickoff. That implies panic. Don't boot the ball like a madman. If there's no defender around to grab the ball out of the net, calmly retrieve it yourself and pass or toss it upfield.

Body language that conveys a negative frame of mind—such as a slouch or a sulky grimace—sends a depressing message to teammates and an inspiring one to opponents. And such gestures only delay the keeper's own recovery. Keepers need to assume a poker face after conceding a goal—and they must put the setback out of their mind, whether or not the goal was scored because of their own error.

TIM HOWARD: BE YOUR OWN HARSHEST CRITIC

All goalkeepers, including the greatest ones ever, have conceded goals that they know they could have stopped. American Tim Howard, who attained status as a world-class goalkeeper in the English Premier League, is far better known for his great saves, but he's let in a few goals that prompted scorching headlines from the British tabloids.

"You have to have broad shoulders and a thick skin," says Howard. "It's a black-and-white position. You either save it or you don't. There's no hiding."

When you're a high-profile professional like Howard, goals conceded will be replayed over and over on television, and sports pundits will all weigh in on whether the goal was the keeper's fault. On talk radio and in Internet chat rooms, fans will also voice their opinions, often in an impolite manner. But a keeper who objectively analyzes his own play makes what others say irrelevant.

"You have to be your own harshest critic," Howard says. "The benefit of holding yourself to the highest standard is that when someone does criticize you, you can look at the situation and say, 'I already knew that' or 'They're completely out of line, and it doesn't matter what they say.' I don't dwell on the good or the bad. If something's broken, I try to fix it. But if it's a one-off type of thing, I take it for what it is and move on.

"I don't overanalyze. When a game ends, I usually know what I did well and what I didn't do well. Every now and again I'll look at something again—not on the highlight shows but within the team and the coaching staff and our video-editing guy—to see how I can improve."

Goalkeepers must be able to cope with a mistake they make during a game. Howard says that this gets easier with experience and age: "In a game, it's difficult to get an error out of your mind, but you have to! It's never easy. With experience, you realize you'll get another play and you'll make it. When I was younger, it weighed on my mind more. But I've learned that one save doesn't make the game. And one mistake doesn't make the game. You'll always have an opportunity to help your team as long as there's still time left."

However, the keeper who has given up a goal should *not* become shy and stop communicating with his teammates to help them organize the defense. The team still needs the direction of the keeper. In addition, focusing on the upcoming play will help the keeper put the conceded goal out of his mind.

Bouncing Back

During a game, the goalkeeper coach can play an important role in helping the keeper bounce back from a setback. One approach is to point out the positive: "You let that goal through, but you did save two point-blank shots." Another approach is to remind the keeper that errors are a part of the game at every level. Struggling keepers need to put out of their mind what they did wrong. They should think about what they did well and how they can continue to help their team.

Afterward, the keeper coach will have a chance to address the errors and the good plays with the keeper. Keepers need to learn from their mistakes, and they can build confidence from recalling what they did well. When a keeper has just had a tough outing, I often tell the keeper to look at the overall performance:

"You didn't play your best game, but you gave your team a chance to win when you stopped that breakaway and kept the score within reach."

Sometimes I don't even bring up the mistakes. If the keeper made errors but we've recently had some really good training, I leave it alone. There's no sense in bringing up errors if the keeper is training well. I may just touch on it and say, "Hey look, you know what? That mess is behind you. Look how good you've been at training." And I leave it at that. Goalkeepers have to develop a short and somewhat selective memory, and the keeper coach can help them do that.

The time and place to examine and correct errors and to rebuild confidence is in training. (See "Correcting Mistakes" in chapter 3.) Good training instills confidence. It's the best way to get the keeper sharp again.

GETTING READY FOR GAME TIME

The pregame warm-up should be designed to give the goalkeeper maximum confidence for the game. It should involve exercises that prepare the keeper for every challenge the game will bring. At all levels, the exercises before kickoff should be ones that the keeper believes will make him successful. The keeper should be feeling invincible after his warm-up. Using exercises that the keeper likes will put him in the perfect mind-set. An optimal warm-up is one that gets the keeper ready to go—physically and mentally. When the opening whistle blows, we want a keeper who is focused and self-assured.

Work Together

Who should choose the exercises to be used in a warm-up? Several factors play into answering this question. The first is the experience level of the keeper. If you are training professional keepers, their warm-ups should be their own. They have played in many matches and have been successful, so they know what they need. Well in advance of the match, the keeper coach should meet with the keeper and find out what exercises he wants to use in his pregame warm-up. Remember that the goal is for the keeper—not the coach—to feel comfortable. The coach can make suggestions, but ultimately it comes down to individual keeper preference.

If the keeper is less experienced, then the coach should guide the keeper on what exercises to use. The coach and the keeper should have a conversation about what will make the keeper feel most prepared and confident for the match. Once that is established, the coach can suggest specific exercises. Regardless of the keeper, the exercises need to replicate the actual movements that the keeper will use in the game.

Length of the Warm-Up

To determine how long the warm-up should last, the goalkeeper coach must know the keeper. Some keepers like a long, slow warm-up—one in which they can take their time and not feel rushed. Other keepers may want a quick, high-tempo warm-up so they have time to settle down before the start of the match. Neither approach is wrong.

CREATING POSITIVE ENERGY

It's perfectly normal to feel nervous before a game, but keepers need to clear their head of negative thoughts. How they go about doing this depends on the individual.

A good goalkeeper coach learns to read his players well enough to know whether to step in—and to know what to say. If a keeper needs a little confidence boost, the coach might provide a positive memory: "This field reminds me of where we beat the Lions SC and you saved the last-minute penalty kick. Remember that?"

If the keeper needs more of a pep talk, the coach might be more direct: "You had great practices this week. You made incredible saves and snatched crosses better than ever. You're as prepared as you can be. Now go out there and have some fun!"

If the keeper needs to rein in his racing mind and relax in the minutes before the game, the coach might initiate some light-hearted conversation: "Hey, Sam, look at the face paint on those fans!"

A keeper who thrives on intensity may be best left alone.

A keeper who struggles with self-doubt can mentally walk through scenarios such as the following: Take a few seconds to scan the field. Imagine a counterattack that results in a breakaway, and you grab the ball from the forward's feet with a perfectly timed dive. Imagine great saves and safely gathered crosses. To clear your head, picture the soccer ball. Try thinking of nothing but that ball. Tell yourself "That ball will be mine!"

The coach should know the keeper's anxiety level before the match, which can be assessed by keen observation. Compare the keeper's behavior before the game to what that keeper is like when you've seen him in a relaxed and confident state.

The keeper who needs to burn off some nervous energy may require a longer warm-up, or one that gets his heart rate up. If the keeper is a veteran and is not anxious or prone to nerves, then he may prefer a short, simple warm-up.

Some keepers like to get out early and "feel" their surroundings, while others prefer to hold back until closer to game time. A young keeper may get ready quickly, whereas an older keeper might need more time to get warm. The important thing is to know and respect what your keeper needs!

Some other factors will also affect the length of a warm-up. The first is the weather. On a cold day, a warm-up may be extended to ensure that the keeper has broken a sweat and is ready to play. If it is a hot day, the warm-up may be cut short to help the goalkeeper keep his energy level high. On hot days, keepers will loosen up more quickly. If you are either extending or decreasing a warm-up, the exercises used should remain the same. The number of repetitions will change in accordance with the weather conditions.

Also, at the highest levels, the time allowed on the game field for warm-ups may be limited. In international and professional competition, the keepers usually get 25 minutes on the field to warm up. This is always enough time to get your work completed properly. If a keeper needs more time, he should do all his running and stretching before coming out onto the field. That way the time on the field is strictly for his goalkeeping work. When time is limited, the keeper, the coach, and the second keeper need to be in perfect sync so that no minutes are wasted. The exercises should be well rehearsed and should flow seamlessly from one to the other.

Key Warm-Up Exercises

The warm-up should cover all challenges that the goalkeeper will face in the game. Start with simple saves, aiming the ball at the keeper so she starts feeling comfortable grasping the ball. Then progress to the more difficult ball collecting that requires more footwork and positioning.

Regardless of the keeper, the warm-up needs to include the following:

- Volleys or drop kicks for the goalkeeper to handle
- Stationary low balls (the keeper is on the ground and just rocks up and down to save low balls)
- Mid-range balls served out of the hand
- Shots from angles
- Shots from distance
- Crosses from deep, corner flag area
- Crosses from high, up the touchline
- Back passes: first-time clearance, two-touch blocks
- Punts, drop kicks, and sidewinder volleys
- Anything that the keeper thinks will help him to be prepared to play

Exercises should be done after the keeper has performed his running and stretching. See chapter 3 for a sample pregame warm-up regimen. The following confidence-building exercises can be used in practice or as part of a pregame warm-up.

Confidence-Building Exercises

Lateral Footwork: Side Step

This exercise hones technique for saving a low or mid-range ball, incorporating footwork, body shape, handling, and saving skills. The service should make the keeper stretch—but not stretch full out and not to the point of risking injury or undermining confidence.

Setup

Place three cones 1 yard apart in a straight horizontal line. Place a flag at each end of the line to form two goals; each flag should be placed 5 yards away from the end cone so that each goal is 5 yards in width. The keeper begins at the goal at one end of the line. A server stands about 6 to 8 yards from the center cone, or if two servers are used, one stands 6 to 8 yards from each goal.

Procedure

The keeper stands at one end of the line of cones. The keeper receives a low volley service from the (first) server, sends it back to the server, then sidesteps over the cones. On reaching the goal at the opposite end of the line from where he started, the keeper receives a low service and returns it. The keeper then jogs back to the other goal and begins again.

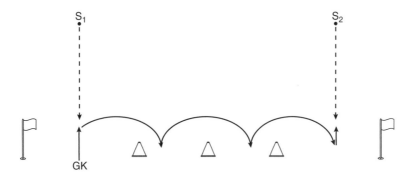

Repetitions

After the keeper makes three to five trips across, the servers send mid-range shots.

Variations

Have the servers send drop kicks and balls off the ground (low and mid-range balls).

Rhythm Work: Two Servers

This exercise gets the goalkeeper used to adjusting properly to low and mid-range balls. It requires two servers.

Setup

The goalkeeper sets up in the goal. Server 1 stands 6 to 8 yards in front of the keeper. Server 2 stands a few yards to the side of server 1.

Procedure

Server 1 sends a volley to the goalkeeper to save high. After the goalkeeper returns the ball to server 1, server 2 sends a low or mid-range (waist-level) ball to the goalkeeper. After making the save, the keeper returns the ball to server 2. Server 1 then serves a low or mid-range ball for the keeper to save, and the cycle continues with the keeper alternately making high and low saves.

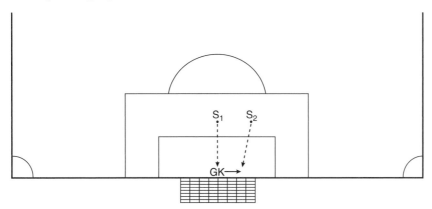

Repetitions

Continue until the keeper has saved four balls from each server.

(continued)

Rhythm Work: Three Servers

Setup

The goalkeeper sets up in the goal. Server 1 stands behind the edge of the goal area and in front of the keeper. Server 2 stands a few yards to one side of server 1 with four balls; server 3 stands a few yards to the other side with another four balls.

Procedure

Server 1 hits a volley to the goalkeeper. The keeper returns the ball to server 1 and immediately saves a low or mid-range ball from server 2. The goalkeeper returns another volley to server 1, then quickly saves a low ball from server 3. Server 1 hits another volley to the keeper, and the cycle repeats.

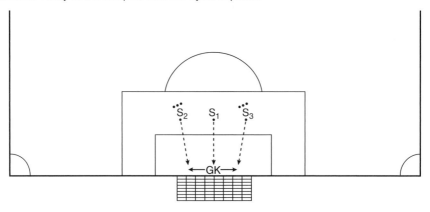

Repetitions

Continue until the keeper has saved four balls each from servers 2 and 3 in addition to returning the volleys from server 1.

Near-Post Coverage

Setup

The goalkeeper starts at the front edge of the goal area. Server 1 stands in front of the goal, about 6 yards behind the edge of the goal area. Server 2 aligns with or is just past the left post, a few yards beyond the edge of the goal area.

Procedure

Server 1 sends a volley to the keeper, who returns it. Server 2 serves a low to mid-range ball just inside the post. The keeper saves it and returns it. Server 1 serves a low to mid-range ball for the keeper to save, and the cycle continues.

Repetitions

When the keeper has saved four shots from each server, server 2 moves to the other post, and the keeper again saves four balls from each server.

Variations

Place three cones between the goalkeeper's starting spot and the spot where the near-post save will be made. The keeper must sidestep over the cones between saves.

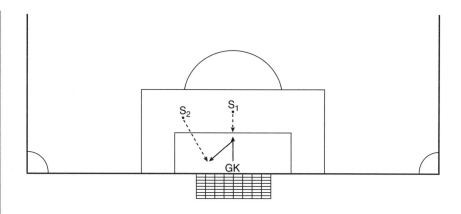

Forward Footwork

Setup

Place five cones in a T formation: three cones 1 yard apart in a vertical line and then two cones 2 yards below and horizontal to the vertical line of cones to form a goal 5 yards wide. The keeper begins at the top of the line of cones. Server 1 lines up inside and about 6 yards behind the cone goal; server 2 lines up on the other side of the cone goal.

Procedure

The keeper shuffles through the three cones and then steps into the goal. Server 1 sends a volley to the keeper, and the keeper sends it back. Server 2 sends a low or mid-range ball to the goal, and the keeper saves it and sends it back. The goalkeeper returns to the top of the line of cones, and the cycle repeats.

Repetitions

After the keeper has saved four shots, server 2 moves to the opposite side, and the keeper saves four more shots.

Variations

The exercise can be done with only one server, who sends balls from both sides.

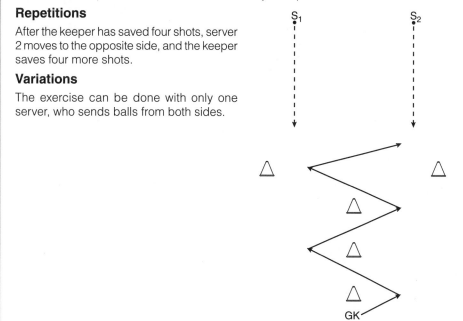

TIM HOWARD'S PREGAME APPROACH

Tim Howard made his Major League Soccer debut at age 19, and at age 21, he became the youngest player to win MLS's Goalkeeper of the Year Award. By the time he hit his 25th birthday, he was starting for Manchester United, playing in stadiums packed with more than 70,000 people for games watched by tens of millions on television. With the U.S. national team, he's lined up against the likes of Brazil, Spain, and Argentina. Howard started in all of the U.S. Team's games at the 2010 World Cup. His precise toss sparked the counterattack that led to Landon Donovan's dramatic stoppage-time goal against Algeria that clinched passage into the second round. So how does he get ready for a game?

"Whether it's a cup final or an exhibition," says Howard, "everything I do is 100 percent the same. No matter who the opponent is, I never take it lightly. I eat the same way, sleep the same way, get the same amount of massages. My warm-up is always the same."

In 2006, Howard moved from Manchester United to Everton. During the 2008 to 2009 season, he set the Everton club record for most shutouts in a season at 17. Howard starts thinking about his next game about 24 hours before kickoff. "I'll visualize good things that I might do during the game," he says. "I imagine myself making saves. I might think about good saves I've made in the past."

Daily Mail/Zuma Press/Icon SMI

Tim Howard, playing for Everton, beats Liverpool's Maxi Rodriguez to the ball.

Some goalkeepers have formal visualization routines that involve sitting down and going through a series of images of the keeper having success on the field. Howard's approach is looser. "I'm a dreamer," he said. "I take my mind to the nice places. But I don't sit down and meditate about the upcoming game. Off and on as the game approaches, I visualize myself doing well."

Coach's Role in the Warm-Up

With a veteran keeper or a young keeper, the coach's role is that of a facilitator. The coach needs to know the routine of the warm-up. Besides the natural order of starting with simpler saves and progressing to the more difficult ones, the coach should be familiar with any specific preferences the keeper has. The order of exercises should be second nature. A keeper should never have to tell his coach what comes next. The coach must understand and work at the pace that the keeper prefers for the warm-up.

The coach needs to be a perfect server of the ball. The coach must hit the target, hit it with the proper pace, and give the keeper the ability to make the save.

If a keeper wants five shots, all five need to be on target. All five need to be savable. All five need to be hit with proper pace. The same is true for crosses. They need to be hit so the keeper can get a feel for the lights, for the rhythm of his technique, and for how the ball may travel in the wind.

Poor service can absolutely destroy a warm-up and shake the confidence of the keeper. For this reason, the coach needs to serve the ball, and this task should not be assigned to a field player. The field player's mind-set is to score. That is not what you want in the warm-up. You want saves! The coach needs to provide the keeper with confidence. To do this, the coach's ability to serve properly is key.

Give the keeper space after he has completed his warm-up and is in a good frame of mind. At that point, I ask the keeper if he needs anything else, and then I simply wish him luck. My job is done. If I fill him with words or thoughts, I run the risk of disrupting his concentration. All the tactical preparation has been discussed earlier, and nothing needs to be said now. It is the keeper's time.

Role of the Second Keeper

My personal preference is to have the second keeper involved in the starter's warm-up. However, this should be the starting keeper's choice. If the starter chooses to involve the second keeper, the second keeper must have the same mentality as the coach and must be ready to act as facilitator. The second keeper must be a good server, and she must know the routine and tempo.

Including the second keeper in the warm-up encourages this player to feel as if she is a part of the starting keeper's performance. This is a positive thing. The second keeper might not partake in the entire warm-up. If that is the case, she can use the rest of the time to warm up (run and stretch) on her own.

If the starting keeper chooses not to include the second keeper, that is OK. As a coach, you need to meet with the second keeper and explain what you would like her to be doing while you are working with the first keeper.

Once the coach has finished warming up the starting keeper, the coach needs to turn his attention to the second keeper. The coach should try to get in as much of a warm-up as possible for this keeper. This is important for two reasons. First, the second keeper will always be in goal for the shooting by the field players as they finish their warm-up. To avoid injury, the keeper should be warm enough to handle shots. The second reason is much more important. What happens if the first keeper suffers an injury? The reserve keeper may need to take over in the goal at a moment's notice. If she's had a proper warm-up and some personal attention, she'll be ready.

PREPARATION PAYS OFF

As a goalkeeper coach with the Kansas City Wizards, I would always bring out the number two and number three keepers for some work before the starting keeper's warm-up. This was beneficial on a number of levels. Any day that the reserve keepers didn't get in any work was essentially a day off; by doing some warm-up work, they were able to stay at the same training rhythm as the starting keeper. Then if something happened to the first keeper, our second keeper was totally prepared to play in a match.

This happened in the 2004 playoffs when the Wizards were playing against the San Jose Earthquakes. During the warm-up, our starting keeper's Achilles tendon became inflamed and forced him out of the lineup. Our second keeper, Bo Oshoniyi, fresh off a solid training session before the match, came in and played a fantastic match. He was ready from the start and made several key saves early in the game. We won the match 3-0, and Bo was outstanding. His preparation in the pregame warm-up was a key factor that allowed him to play at such a high level.

Have a Backup Plan

Goalkeepers are creatures of habit and routine. They know what they like, especially before a match, so you shouldn't mess with their routine. However, unusual and unexpected things sometimes happen, and adjustments must be made.

For example, you might not be allowed on the field before the match; if this is the case, your warm-up may need to be performed in a hallway, on a track, or on a small patch of grass. You may arrive late, or your opponents may arrive late, delaying the game. You may encounter bad field conditions.

Try to nail things down in advance in order to avoid surprises. Generate ideas about how to change things up if the unexpected occurs. If you've thought ahead about how you might deal with changes in the routine, you can respond to changes calmly. Meet with your keepers before arrival at the field, and explain to them what has changed. Make suggestions for how you *will* make it work. Adapt to the situation. Avoid panic and you will be successful.

Coach and Keeper: Building a Unique Partnership

Among the many ways that goalkeepers differ from their teammates is that they have a coach dedicated to their position. Even at the youth level, clubs often have keeper coaches or trainers to work with goalies. The keeper coach ensures that goalkeepers are receiving the proper training—that is, training that improves their skills and keeps them fit. This coach also helps the keepers comprehend all facets of the game. In addition, the keeper coach is responsible for motivating keepers and helping them overcome setbacks.

The keeper coach and all the keepers—whether they're starters or back-ups—need to establish and maintain a solid relationship. Teammate support notwithstanding, when the going gets rough, the keeper will sometimes feel as if she's all alone. At those times, knowing that the coach is always in her corner can make all the difference.

Keeper coaches should establish a bond with their keepers by having frequent conversations with them and by closely observing them to learn what kind of approach they respond to best. The keeper coach should be able to build a keeper's confidence after setbacks and help the keeper put success in perspective. "My door is always open" should be the keeper coach's motto. Keepers need to feel comfortable coming to the keeper coach to discuss any problems they might have, even if those problems involve other coaches or their teammates.

APPRECIATE DIFFERENT PERSONALITIES

When it comes to motivating players, there may be nothing more important in coaching than realizing that different people react differently to various approaches. It may take some trial and error and some patience, but after a few practice sessions, attentive coaches will have an idea of how to get the best from their players.

Harsh criticism may bring out the best in one player but may crush another. Tim Howard is a good example. When I coached him at a young age, I was very hard on him because I knew he could handle it. And that approach motivated him. He liked it. He responded well when I was demanding and hard on him, and I didn't have to always put my arm around him.

I've had keepers whom I could be very frank with. With these keepers, I could say, "Hey, that was terrible." They could handle it and move on, and it spurred them to do well. But I've had other young keepers whom I had to constantly pump up and make feel good. I've had older keepers who knew exactly when they erred and why. There was no need to point out their mistakes. That's the art of coaching: knowing what motivates which players and how you can talk to them.

A HEALTHY, OPEN RELATIONSHIP

Wade Jackson/Icon SMI

Having played for pro clubs in four different nations, former U.S. national team goalkeeper Kasey Keller had his share of goalkeeper coaches. His keeper coach while on U.S. duty was Milutin Soskic, who served the United States at the 1994, 1998, 2002, and 2006 World Cups (Keller was a part of the latter three squads).

Soskic, who helped Yugoslavia finish fourth at the 1962 World Cup, was considered the world's best keeper in the early 1960s along with the Soviet Union's Lev Yashin. Keller described to us in a 1998 interview why he felt so comfortable training with Soskic: "He listens to you. He's not someone who says, 'This is the way you have to do it, because this is how I did it.' He's here to work for us and he realizes that. He doesn't push you into things. He's here to get you ready to play a game and he does that."

Tim Howard, Keller's successor as the U.S. team's number one keeper, agrees that a good goalkeeper–keeper coach relationship requires give-and-take. "It should be a healthy, open relationship," he says. "You're bouncing ideas off each other more often than a field player and an assistant coach. It's more about compatibility."

Howard says that he made a smooth adjustment to keeper coaches when he moved from MLS to England. "When I went to Manchester United at age 23, I wasn't going to tell anybody a whole

Kasey Keller, shown here defending a high shot by Latvia during an international friendly match in preparation for the 2006 World Cup, thrived under coach Milutin Soskic.

lot of anything," he said. "I was gonna shut up and basically let the goalkeeper coach have the reins. But as I got more and more experience, certain situations I went into I commanded more respect. It was mutual respect. I felt I had more liberty to share ideas about what I thought was right for me." Goalkeepers should speak to their goalkeeper coaches to air their ideas, but also have an open mind to what the coaches' ideas are.

When I first started coaching, I was probably too aggressive and "in your face." I would use comments such as "That wasn't good enough!" "That needs to be much better!" and "What the hell was that?!" As I've gotten older and gained experience and confidence, I've become more lenient regarding errors because I know I can correct them in training. I've also learned that taking a less adversarial approach is generally more effective. Good training goes much, much further than sharp words in helping players improve. When flaws need to be discussed, be honest but not overly critical. As mentioned in chapter 2, throwing in a positive comment along with a negative one is always a good idea.

TRAINER VERSUS COACH

In terms of goalkeeping, a trainer is a person who develops the exercises and puts keepers through their paces. A coach does this as well, but also offers insight into the keepers' actions in the goal. Most coaches and trainers perform both roles.

At the youngest levels, you are more of a coach, developing and correcting the technical and tactical responsibilities of the keeper. In dealing with more senior keepers, your role is more that of a trainer, but you must also continue to coach. Even a very experienced keeper will benefit from a keeper coach's scouting report. And a good keeper coach will notice when the veteran keeper needs extra work on a particular part of his game.

All keepers must be trained or coached with an attitude that they are playing in a real match—that is, training should simulate game situations. Whether you consider yourself a coach or a trainer, you should include these basics in every training session:

- Take into account the types of plays and balls that the keeper will deal with during the course of the match.
- Vary the distance and the angles of the service as well as the service itself.
- Include balls off the ground, half volleys, volleys, and crosses (in-swinging and outswinging crosses).

DAY-TO-DAY TRAINING

In addition to having a good relationship with her keepers, the goalkeeper coach needs to be extremely knowledgeable about the position. This coach must be someone the head coach can trust to get the most out of the keepers. The keeper coach needs to be organized; she must know how to plan a session, know how to run a session, and fully comprehend the objectives of the session.

Being in Tune With the Head Coach

A primary role of the goalkeeper coach is to make sure the head coach's strategies and tactics are relayed to the goalkeeper—and that the goalkeeper completely comprehends how the team plans to play. You don't want the goalkeeper organizing the team one way while the head coach wants a different approach.

Daily communication must take place between the head coach and the goalkeeper coach. These conversations need to be open and honest, with a mutual sharing of information. The keeper coach must synchronize the specialized keeper training with that of the team. To plan out the session, the goalkeeper coach must know how much time he'll have with the goalkeepers in training before they join the rest of the team. The keeper coach also needs to know if all the keepers will be involved in the team training, and if not, who is staying for extra specialized training.

In addition, the keeper coach must know what the keepers will be facing when they train with the team. For example, if the keeper coach learns that there will be a crossing-and-finishing session, the keepers' individual training will include warming up the technical areas that will prepare the keepers for that activity. If the head coach tells the keeper coach that there will be an emphasis on tactical training without much shooting on goal, the keeper coach may then include more shot stopping in the individual session. Or he might ask the head coach to provide field players for 15 minutes after practice for shots on the keepers.

The head coach will also pass along to the keeper coach tactical issues that need to be worked on with the keepers. For example, the head coach may have a concern that the back line isn't moving forward in unison. The keeper coach might relay the following to the keeper: "Keep an eye on the right back. Make sure he's not keeping forwards onside when we're going 6v4 today."

In turn, the keeper coach must share information with the head coach about the keepers so that the head coach can make appropriate plans and take any necessary action. The keeper coach should convey how the keepers are performing, which keeper is in the best form, and whether there are any problems with the mentality of the keepers.

Working With Field Players

The keeper coach and the keepers must also have a good working relationship with the field players. To ensure that they are all on the same page, the goalkeeper coach should either run or participate in the functional training of the defending players and the goalkeeper. The proper organization between the defending players and the keeper is paramount to any successful team.

The goalkeeper coach can incorporate tactical concerns that the keeper might face in a match. Functional training should consist of exercises involving the back four and the midfield players (6v4). It should also address the keeper's role in the buildup of the attack. During these shared exercises, many questions will be answered, and concerns will be corrected.

Planning and Organizing

The importance of planning and organizing cannot be overstated. Practice time is too precious to waste. By the time the keepers step on the field, the keeper coach should know exactly how they'll be spending every minute of the practice.

Before each practice, I ask myself the following questions:

- How am I going to get all the keepers involved?
- How am I going to keep them all active?
- What kind of training do my keepers need at this stage of the week? At this stage of the season?
- Who's going to get the priority during the training?

For a practice session before a game, for example, the coach needs to balance getting the prospective starter ready for the match with providing optimal training for the backups.

Obviously, the keeper coach must design the training to help the keepers improve at all aspects of the position and must put the keepers through sessions that expose their weaknesses. At the same time, the keeper coach shouldn't impose his will on the keeper so much that it takes away from the keeper's confidence. If a goalkeeper struggles with a particular session, it might be good to follow up with a "go-to exercise."

Goalkeepers like certain exercises because those exercises give them confidence. It's the keeper coach's job to find those exercises and to keep those exercises in the daily training. Figure out what each keeper's go-to exercise is. This is the exercise that a keeper can always fall back on to get her in the groove and to help her do well in the other areas.

With younger keepers, such as the U17 national team players, I'll physically push the envelope on Monday, Tuesday, and Wednesday (with a match on Saturday) because the players are young and usually need to work through some things to get themselves ready.

With older keepers, I may get after them on Monday or Tuesday, and then evaluate their state. If they're feeling good and feeling confident, I may just let it ride and keep using exercises that give them confidence.

CORRECTING MISTAKES

What you decide to emphasize during training sessions will depend in part on how the keeper performed in the last game. If a keeper blundered badly, the keeper coach must help rebuild confidence. If the error was simply a lapse of concentration, then it's wise not to dwell on the mistake.

But if the keeper, for example, mistimed a cross or was stuck to his line when he should have intercepted the cross, that facet of the game can be emphasized in training the week after the game. It won't be the sole focus, but it will be a focus.

You should also have an upfront and honest conversation with the keeper about the mistakes he made and how to correct them. Video always helps. If a goalkeeper has excuses for why the goal was conceded—claiming that this happened or that happened—the video reveals exactly what went down. Watch the video with the keeper and talk about the incident and how to handle a similar situation. Then tell the keeper, "Let's make sure we take care of it during training this week."

A portion of the training early in the week will be designed to make sure that mistakes are erased. If the problem was that the keeper didn't come out for the cross, you should plan sessions designed to demonstrate to the keeper that he can—and how he can—meet the cross.

KNOW THY KEEPER

Coaches must adjust their approach to the individual. Some keepers might need the soft touch to get in the right frame of mind. Others might require a rousing pep talk.

Some keepers might fall apart if they are given a direct, honest critique without plenty of compliments to go with it. Others are fine with a harsh, straightforward assessment. So how does the coach know what's best for each individual?

It starts with close observation. The coach pays attention to the players at every practice and game, as well as off the field. After a keeper has a poor outing, recall what the warm-up was like and what your pregame conversations entailed. If the keeper had a standout game, ask yourself the following: What did we do before that match? If the keeper had a real nervous outing, try to recall what the pregame was like that time. You might even keep a notebook that details your training sessions and reminds you of what you've been telling a keeper.

Don't be afraid to seek advice from others, such as the players' previous coaches. They might provide valuable insight. And above all, speak with your keepers. Get to know them. Ask them about their off-the-field life. Find out if they have any worries about family, school, and so on. Let them know you care about them. If something is bothering your keeper—maybe his girlfriend just broke up with him—talking about it might help him clear his head and get ready to focus on the play.

Find out if your keepers have any issues with other coaches or teammates. The more information you gather, the easier it will be to get your keepers on the right track—and you'll be forging a solid relationship with your keepers.

Honesty solves a lot of problems. So get feedback constantly. A week into the season, ask the keepers to voice their opinions on practices and your coaching. This doesn't mean you always have to make changes, but you'll gain the keepers' respect, and perhaps you'll identify something that might be done differently.

GIVING IT YOUR BEST SHOT

To properly train a goalkeeper, the keeper coach must have an accurate shot. Being able to place the ball wherever you want is crucial because you need to train your keepers to stop shots anywhere on the frame. As a keeper coach, you must also be able to strike the ball so that it moves in various ways—bending or flat—and at different paces.

Most goalkeeper coaches get better and better at shooting simply because they shoot so often. But if you're a coach and you notice too many of your shots flying in directions you didn't intend—balls are flying high and wide—you need to hone your shooting skills. This means taking the time to practice shooting against a wall, over and over again, until your shot is as good as a forward's.

One way to improve your shooting skills is to grab a ball bag and line up shots from the penalty spot. Practice aiming at particular locations on the net as you focus on pace and accuracy. Keeper coaches must be able to strike the ball at various speeds.

The same goes for the keepers themselves. Keepers obviously need good foot skills to play the position well, but they also need these skills so they can train each other. Keeping goalkeepers involved in field play during training helps them improve their foot skills. But extra shooting training may be required.

PICKING THE STARTER

The keeper coach must support the head coach's decision on who will start and on any other team issues. Private discussions and disagreements can occur, but in front of the team the keeper coach must fully support all decisions by the head coach.

The Keeper Coach and the Backups

The reserve keepers could be called on at any time, whether it's because of an injury or a red card. Today's backup keeper could be tomorrow's star. The keeper coach must treat the backups with respect, make them feel like part of the team, and help them improve. The goalkeeper coach must have a systematic approach throughout the season for the second keeper. Reserve keepers must take steps to develop competition-level readiness in four key areas.

Technical Sharpness

1. Perform 2 to 4 additional bouts (sets) of exercises to increase fitness.
2. Practice handling and catching, low to mid-range balls, shot stopping, crosses, and distribution with the feet.

Match Preparation

1. Stay tactically in tune with the team game plan.
2. Treat all training matches with the same competitive spirit as a real game.
3. Play reserve matches with the supervision of the keeper coach.
4. Stay engaged and ready to start or replace the starter if needed.

Mental Preparation

1. Attend all team meetings.
2. Analyze scouting reports and video.
3. Participate in prematch warm-ups.
4. Monitor the conversation and analysis during the match.

Physical Preparation

1. Maintain a high level of anaerobic fitness.
2. Train lightly the day of the match.
3. Limit days off from training.
4. Perform appropriate weight training (see chapter 12).

The goalkeeper coach must have a clear vision of who the number one goalkeeper should be, must know his reasons for his choice ("Johnny should start because of X, Y, and Z"), and must be able to present his case to the head coach. However, sometimes the head coach will choose a different starter from the one recommended by the keeper coach. If this occurs, the two coaches should certainly discuss the issue, but when the keeper coach leaves the room, he should support the head coach's decision.

Then comes the tough part: The goalkeeper coach is always the guy who tells the keeper he's not playing. If the head coach picked a different starter than you (the keeper coach) preferred, you should *not* let the players know this. Never say, "If it were up to me, you'd be playing." Take that out of the equation.

How the bad news is presented to the reserve keepers can go a long way toward maintaining a good relationship between the goalkeepers. The keeper coach should be frank: "You're not playing. Here's who's playing. Here's the reason why. I know it's disappointing. I don't expect you to be happy about it. We'll keep getting after it in training. When your time comes, you'll get your chance to get in there and do the job."

Coaches should not pit goalkeepers against each other. The keepers must be good teammates, not adversaries. Of course, the keepers know that they're competing with each other. When talking to the keeper who didn't get the start, you should stress that the only way to get into the lineup is through good training.

You may want to point out a specific reason why one goalkeeper is preferred over the other. For example, a keeper coach may tell the backup that the other guy was picked because "he's coming off his line better than you are." This identifies a clear reason, and it gives the keeper something to focus on in training. Goalkeepers will appreciate a specific reason. They will react better to that than if you simply say, "He's starting because we say he is." This type of statement is more likely to create animosity between the team's keepers.

The keeper coach must be prepared to give clear answers on how the keeper who is not starting can improve. And the coach should emphasize that he's willing to work with the keeper on those deficiencies. As a keeper coach, you can't guarantee that a backup keeper is going to win the starting job; however, you can let the keeper know that you'll help him close the gap so he'll have a better chance of keeping the job if he does get to play.

PREPARING THE STARTER— NOTHING BUT SAVES

Assuming that the team plays weekend games, the practices early in the week— Monday, Tuesday, and Wednesday—will be the time when the keepers are pushed the hardest and when the keeper coach addresses deficiencies. But in training the day before the game, there should be nothing but success for the goalkeeper.

In the keeper training sessions the day before a game, all the shots must be at and around the keeper. Focus on the clean handling of shots, and make sure the sessions are not long. If the keeper makes four of five good saves, it's time to stop and get someone else in the goal. That way, the starting keeper walks out of there thinking, *Hey, I just had the cleanest day of my life.* The starter should leave practice believing that there's no way he'll give up a goal in the next day's game.

The start of the pregame warm-up does not need to be done in front of the goal, and doing it away from the goal has some advantages. Sometimes the goal—or even the field—isn't available for warm-ups, so it's good to get the keepers accustomed to warming up away from the goal. Also, when goalkeepers begin their warm-up away from the goal, they can more easily focus on getting warm rather than preventing goals.

The pace should be determined by the goalkeeper. The service should be accurate, should require different kinds of catching, and should ensure success. Keepers should stretch and relax between series. They should let the coach know how much time they want between series; the coach keeps track of how much time they have to warm up before game time.

Pregame Warm-up Progression

Catching Volleys

Setup

Place two cones 5 yards apart to simulate a goal. The goalkeeper begins between the cones. Servers stand about 6 yards in front of each cone; each server has a supply of balls.

Procedure

The goalkeeper saves a chest-high volley from server 1. The keeper moves across the width of the cones and saves a chest-high volley from server 2. After 8 to 10 chest-high volleys (or the keeper's preferred number of volleys), repeat the set with drop kicks, and then repeat it again with shots off the ground.

Variations

Using two servers is a good way to keep the reserve goalkeeper involved. But this exercise can also be done with one server; the server stands 6 yards away, centered between the cones.

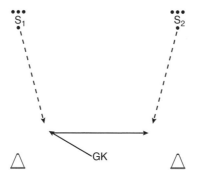

(continued)

Stationary Low Saves

This exercise helps the keeper loosen up and prepare for the rigors of match saves. The keeper's movements will resemble those of a windshield wiper: starting low, going up, and coming back down.

Setup

Place two cones 5 yards apart to simulate a goal. The goalkeeper begins between the cones. A server stands about 6 yards in front of the keeper, centered between the cones; the server has a supply of balls.

Procedure

The goalkeeper starts on his side on the ground, holding the ball as if he had just made a save (*a*). The keeper rolls the ball back to the server while rocking onto his hip (*b*). The server delivers a firm ball back into the keeper's hands (*c*) as the keeper falls back to the ground. Repeat 8 to 10 times.

Hitting the Ground—Mid-range Volleys

In this exercise, the keeper works on hitting the ground in a controlled fashion.

Setup

Place two cones 5 yards apart to simulate a goal. The goalkeeper begins between the cones. A server stands about 6 yards in front of the keeper, centered between the cones; the server has a supply of balls.

Procedure

The server delivers a straight volley for the goalkeeper to handle. The goalkeeper returns the ball to the server. The server kicks a ball out of his hands at hip height to the keeper's right. The keeper catches the ball and falls into a mid-range save. The keeper then returns to the middle and prepares for a delivery to the left. The server tosses the ball to the keeper's left. Repeat the sequence three times for a total of six saves on each side.

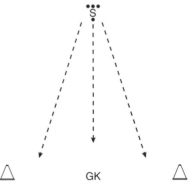

Getting Into Rhythm

This exercise gets the keepers moving and hones their footwork skills and their ability to adjust to balls of different heights.

Setup

Place two cones 5 yards apart to simulate a goal. The goalkeeper begins between the cones. Two servers stand a few yards apart and about 6 yards in front of the keeper.

Procedure

The goalkeeper saves a volley from server 1 *(a)*. The keeper immediately returns the ball and then shuffles over to meet a low ball from server 2 *(b)*. The keeper continues until server 2 has sent four balls. Then the servers switch roles and positions, and the keeper saves four more low balls on the other side. Repeat the complete sequence on both sides with the second server delivering mid-range (waist-level) shots off the ground.

Angle Saves

In this exercise, the keeper prepares for the game by saving shots at different angles, high and low. Services should be driven around the body frame of the goalkeeper. Coaches should get feedback on how many reps the keeper wants. The keeper should choose whether servers take shots from a stationary ball or take a touch before the shot.

(continued)

Setup

The goalkeeper sets up in a regulation goal. Server 1 is inside the penalty area about 6 yards to the side of the post, between the edge of the goal area and the penalty area. Server 2 is at the edge of the D (where the penalty arc meets the penalty area).

Procedure

The goalkeeper saves a shot from server 1. The keeper then moves over to save a shot from server 2. After four to six saves, reverse the order of delivery so that the keeper is moving to the opposite side. Then move to the other side of the goal and repeat the entire sequence.

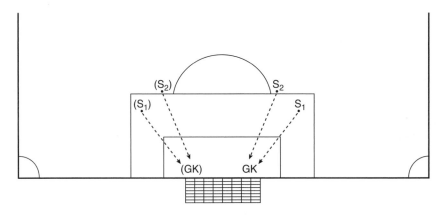

Crossing

Work both sides of the field at once if possible—but leave the decision up to the goalkeeper.

Setup

A server begins at each corner flag. The keeper sets up in goal.

Procedure

Servers take turns sending crosses, and they alternate in-swinging and outswinging crosses. When the keeper has had enough corner-flag crosses, servers move to positions beyond the penalty area and serve crosses aimed farther from the goal. Repeat according to the goalkeeper's personal preference.

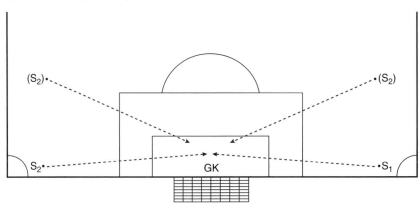

Kicking and Passing

Before the opening whistle, a keeper must get prepared to strike the ball well. In this exercise, the reserve keepers shag balls.

Setup

The keeper begins in the goal. The coach or backup keeper stands about 10 yards out with a supply of balls.

Procedure

The coach and the keeper exchange one-touch passes. When the keeper is ready, the coach hits back passes to the keeper for first-touch clearance *(a)*. The keeper drives the ball upfield *(b)*, warming up both the right foot and the left foot. Repeat, but now the keeper controls the ball with the first touch and then drives it to a target (e.g., a reserve keeper) with the second touch. Continue according to the keeper's personal preference.

Blockouts

In this exercise, the keeper works on foot saves. Keepers may need to use a foot save on an opponent's shot, a deflection, or a wild back pass.

Setup

The keeper begins in the goal. The coach stands about 10 yards out with a supply of balls.

Procedure

The coach plays a fast, hard low ball to the goalkeeper *(a)*. The goalkeeper uses the inside of the foot to block the ball upfield *(b)*. Repeat according to the keeper's preference.

(continued)

Pregame Warmup Progression *(continued)*

Distribution

Setup

The keeper sets up in goal with a supply of balls.

Procedure

The goalkeeper sends several kicks (according to personal preference) of each type—punts, sidewinders, and drop kicks—toward a midfield target.

READY, SET, KICKOFF

The last thing a keeper needs just before game time is to have the crowd get on him when it sees balls fly into the net or to begin to feel insecure because he's missing shots. For that reason, no one should shell the goalkeeper in the warm-up.

The best way for a keeper to be warmed up is to work with someone who understands the keeper's mentality. Therefore, the goalkeeper coach or backup keeper (acting on the keeper coach's instructions) should do the shooting. I'm dead set against having teammates shoot on the keeper in the pregame warm-up. Some goalkeepers like it, so you sometimes have to allow it. But the mentality of a field player is not conducive to a good keeper warm-up, because the field player is shooting to score in order to warm up herself.

The shots should be challenging, but as the warm-up goes on, the shooter should make less and less effort to score. And never end on a goal. Always end with a confidence-boosting clean save.

My college coach was not a goalkeeper. He was a forward. When he would warm me up, he would score 30 to 40 goals. When the game started, the last thing I had was confidence. I had just been lit up with 30 goals! I spent the first 20 minutes praying that the ball wouldn't come near me.

Because the goalkeeper is already under enough pressure (she knows that most mistakes lead to a goal), the warm-up has to be clean and confidence building, whether the keeper is young or old. You want the keeper to walk into the game clear of any doubt or problems. Serve accurate and consistent balls to the keeper in the warm-up, and she'll go into the game feeling good.

Goalkeepers are all different, but they tend to be alike in one respect: They like routine. The goalkeeper coach needs to know how long any particular keeper likes to warm up before a game and what makes her sharp and confident. This should be established in advance, so come game day, the keeper coach is in synch with what the goalkeeper wants, and there aren't any hiccups.

Once the warm-up routine is finished, leave the goalkeeper alone with her thoughts. Don't raise the anxiety level before a game by offering a wide range of advice—"Remember this! Remember that! Be ready for this!" If there is something crucial that the keeper should be reminded of, then a concise statement may be appropriate. But usually, you can just say, "Hey, great warm-up. Good luck. See you at halftime." And that's enough.

HALFTIME CONVERSATION

The halftime break gives the keeper coach a chance to relay any important information that the keeper needs to know in order to help the team in the second half. First, the keeper coach should let the keeper decompress, get a drink, and talk to his teammates.

After the head coach addresses the team, the keeper coach can have a conversation with the keeper. I usually ask the keeper if he has any concerns. He might say that the head coach addressed them all. Or the keeper might point out something that wasn't covered. For example, the keeper might say, "We're giving the left midfielder too much space to move down the wings and hit crosses." The keeper coach can then check with the head coach to see if this needs to be discussed with the defenders.

A keeper may ask for feedback. For example, he might ask, "How are my starting spots?" The keeper coach can then assure the keeper that he's playing it right, or the coach may advise him to move farther out or stay closer to his line.

I try to make it a dialogue unless I notice something severe that the keeper needs to correct. If that is the case, I explain what the keeper should be doing differently. This is usually something that comes up more often with younger keepers.

The keeper coach can also offer advice based on the score. If the team is up 1-0, the keeper might be reminded that as the game goes on and his team remains ahead, the opponent is likely to throw more players into the attack and take a more direct approach. The keeper should expect that he might need to direct his defenders to cover the extra players thrown into the attack by the opponent—especially on corner kicks and free kicks.

DON'T HAVE A GOALKEEPER COACH?

Of course, not all teams, especially at the youth level, have the luxury of a goalkeeper coach or goalkeeper trainer. Besides educating themselves on goalkeeper exercises, coaches and keepers can use observation to assess what training is needed. Look at your goalkeeper and ask, "What would I do to score on this keeper?" (The keeper can watch himself on videotape.) If you realize that the keeper is vulnerable to low balls, then find exercises that emphasize low-ball saves.

It's also worthwhile to have a keeper coach come out to one of your practices and work with the keepers. The coaches and the keepers can then repeat the training on their own in future practices. Also, show your goalkeepers how to train each other. On youth teams that have only a head coach and assistant coach, the assistant should make an effort to work with the goalkeepers in practices and in pregame warm-ups.

The coach might also remind the keeper not to rush his distribution while his team has the lead. Likewise, if the team is behind, the keeper should be prepared to distribute the ball in a way that helps his team launch quick attacks as time runs out.

Having done his homework on the opponent, the keeper coach will also be able to warn the keeper of what types of substitutions are likely. Perhaps the opponent tends to bring in a tall, powerful attacker to feed crosses to, or a speedy forward who thrives on defense-splitting passes.

As always, the coach should avoid overloading the player with information. Practical, concise advice is the most helpful.

PERSONAL PREFERENCES

A goalkeeper *must* enter the game with the right frame of mind. And you'll find that different keepers prefer different methods of reaching that mind-set.

When I was an assistant coach at Rutgers in 1989, we reached the NCAA semifinals, where we lost to Tony Meola's University of Virginia team. Our keeper was Dave Barrueta, who, at one point, was the NCAA Division I leader in shutouts.

Dave was the kind of guy who gained confidence by just catching the ball. He just wanted to catch it and feel the ball. He didn't need to fly around. He didn't need to see a lot of shots. He wanted to handle some balls hit from volleys. He wanted to catch some crosses. And if he did that clean, he'd feel very confident.

Our first-round opponent that year was Columbia, and it was a cold day. I was a young coach. It was the NCAA tournament. Obviously, I was very excited. I said, "Look, let's get down there and warm up." Dave responded with, "I just want to warm up for five minutes today."

I said, "Dave, this is crazy. You need a proper warm-up." He replied, "No. I'm so ready mentally, all I need to do is catch a few balls and get the feel of the ball, and I'm ready to play. I don't need anything else today."

I was very uncomfortable at first. That's not how I saw a warm-up. But sometimes you have to trust your goalkeepers, knowing what gets them ready to play and what makes them feel more confident. Sure enough, we won 3-0, and Dave played a very good game.

So for a pregame warm-up, I allow the starting goalkeeper to make the call on what he believes will make him feel ready and sharp for a match. And this will vary.

Peter Schmeichel, the great Danish national team and Manchester United goalkeeper, took a nearly superstitious approach to warming up. He insisted on saving 100 shots before each game.

Tim Howard wanted to see a lot of shots in the warm-up. Meola didn't want to see as many shots; rather, he wanted to do more with his legs to loosen himself up. Brad Guzan is a guy who wants to see some shots and a whole bunch of crosses.

You have to give everybody a bit of what makes them feel confident. It can't be the coach's warm-up. With younger players, the coach needs to provide more guidance, but in general, it should be the keeper's warm-up.

THE GAME IS THERE FOR YOU

Knowing the position inside and out is the key to being good at coaching goalkeepers. Many high-level goalkeeper coaches are former keepers who played the game and studied it for years. But whether or not you're an experienced keeper, a great source for figuring out what goalkeepers need is the game itself. Watching games at all levels will help coaches and players understand the demands of the position and how to prepare for them. When watching games, examine what the successful goalkeepers do, and then try to replicate that in practice!

chapter 4

The Save Starts Before the Shot

Almost everything the goalkeeper does is affected by his body shape before a shot is taken. Even the simpler challenges are complicated if the keeper's body shape isn't optimal. In fact, the biggest problem I see in young goalkeepers is a faulty ready position. When a goalkeeper catches a shot or punches the ball to safety, that's just a small part of the process. The keeper performs the crucial preparation before the shooter unleashes the shot—this preparation involves body shape, footwork, hand positioning, and angle play. If the keeper's body isn't balanced, loose, and poised for action, the keeper's ability to respond will be compromised.

That's why we spend so much time working with keepers to establish a proper stance. Whether the keeper needs to launch his body toward the upper corner of the goal or catch a ball driven at him, the shape he's in before the shot will determine if he can cope with the challenge.

ASSESSING BODY SHAPE FROM THE GROUND UP

The way to coach body shape is from the ground up. Observe the keeper—don't watch the shooter—and progress from the feet to the head. See where the keeper's weight is distributed over the feet, check the width of the stance, and look to see if the knees are straight or bent. Is the back straight or angled forward? Check the height at which the hands are held and the distance between the hands. Are the elbows straight or bent? Does the upper body appear tense or relaxed? Where is the keeper's chin in relation to the rest of the body? The angle of the chin will help you evaluate whether the keeper's body is erect, leaning forward, or leaning backward. Finally, pay attention to the head and the eyes. Is the head moving or stationary? Where are the eyes looking?

Body Shape: Where It All Starts

The proper ready position is a matter of combining all the elements of body shape—from the feet through the legs, to the upper body, and to the head. Assuming the ready position prepares the body for action and encourages the mind to focus on the task at hand.

General Shape

Whenever the ball is within shooting distance, the keeper should assume the correct body position for making a save. Every part of the body, from the feet to the head, contributes to the save.

- The weight is on the balls of the feet. (The ball of the foot is the area just before the toes.)
- The legs are in a comfortable athletic position. (Some keepers are big, so their base stance will be wide.)
- The knees are bent.
- The glutes are down so that the keeper is in a slight squat.
- The back is at a forward-leaning angle.
- The hands are at the sides, in a neutral position. This enables the keeper to move the hands correctly to save balls hit low, medium, or high.
- The elbows are bent.
- The chin is over the toes.
- The upper body is relaxed.
- The head is still.
- The eyes are only on the ball. Keepers catch with the eyes and then the hands.

Coaching Points

- Keepers need to be in this basic stance on most shot-stopping attempts.
- The feet need to be set (stationary) when the ball is hit. All movement should be done before ball contact.
- The hands should move together to make the save. The hands work in pairs.
- Once the ball is struck, the palms should face the ball.
- The body should be behind the ball.

Common Errors

- The feet are flat on the ground. Balance is on the heels, not the balls of the feet. This will limit reaction time, speed, and power.

- The feet are not set (the body is still in motion) when the ball is struck. This will limit the keeper's ability to change direction and to produce speed and power.
- The body is erect. This is a nonathletic position. Therefore, movement will be slow and limited.
- The hands are placed below the waist.* This will limit the keeper's ability to save shots hit with pace at waist height or above. Good forwards will recognize this and punish the keeper.
- The hands are too far apart. This will cause the keeper to give up rebounds because the hands will arrive late at the ball. The hands need to work in pairs.
- The body is stiff, causing the ball to rebound off the keeper.
- The eyes are not focused on the ball all the way into the hands. As a result, balls that should be held will become rebounds in front of the goal.

* In breakaway situations, when the keeper knows the ball will be coming in low, the hands should be held low and away from the body, with the palms forward, to cover more area.

SETTING THE LOWER BODY FOR POWER AND EXPLOSIVENESS

Goalkeepers who stand on their heels lose power and explosion, and they won't be able to pounce as quickly. Keepers in the ready position should be on the balls of their feet, meaning they are resting their weight on the area of the feet where the toes meet the rest of the foot.

The feet must also be the right distance apart. The best way to determine the right distance is to find a comfortable, athletic position. Steadfast rules such as "place the feet shoulder-width apart" should be avoided. Keepers come in different shapes, and this rule might not always result in the best position, especially for large, tall keepers whose stance is naturally wider. Keepers should begin with a stance that is roughly shoulder-width apart, and they should adjust from there to accommodate their particular size and individual preferences. The stance should not restrict movement. I always tell keepers that they should make sure they are comfortable.

With knees slightly bent and the upper body leaning slightly forward, the keeper is ready to spring into action. A keeper can experiment with various degrees of knee flexion and body angle while imagining a shot about to be taken. This helps the keeper find a position that is comfortable and that provides her with the momentum to quickly shift from a stationary position into movement toward the ball.

READYING THE HANDS AND UPPER BODY

Tim Vizer/Icon SMI

Hope Solo demonstrates perfect form while making a save for the St. Louis Athletica.

A lot of coaches who don't specialize in goalkeeping teach goalkeepers to keep their hands below their waist. With this method, the arms are hanging below the waist, which means that the hands will have to travel a long way for any ball that isn't hit low. The farther the hands have to travel, the less likely they are to get to the ball in time. Therefore, keepers should position their hands and elbows at waist height so that the hands can go down and come up with equal ease.

When the keeper is preparing to catch the ball, the elbows should be slightly flexed—not to a degree that the hands are out of position but enough so that the arms can move quickly to the ball. If a keeper is dropping balls, then the elbows are probably not bending. A keeper who tries to make a catch with straight arms won't have the "give" that allows a well-struck ball to be grasped firmly.

Also, the arms should not be spread too far apart. If a keeper is making a lot of one-handed saves or is tipping or parrying balls rather than making solid contact, the hands are probably not being kept close enough to one another. The hands should always work in pairs. The keeper's body shape should enable him to get his hands together when making a save. Even if the ball cannot be caught, two hands make a larger, stronger barrier than one and will be more effective in blocking or redirecting the ball.

The upper body should have a slight forward lean. Reminding keepers to keep the chin over the toes ensures that they lean forward. The upper body must also be relaxed. When preparing for contact, the keeper does not want to be stiff. The muscles will not react quickly enough if the keeper is rigid.

The head should be still, and the eyes, of course, must be focused on the ball. The eyes catch the ball! Meeting the ball with the hands requires tracking the entire path of the shot with the eyes. Taking your eyes off the ball for just a split second can result in a goal because the course of the ball's flight reveals where the ball will arrive. Keepers who don't follow the ball all the way into their hands are the ones who get beat by shots they should have saved.

IT WON'T WORK WITHOUT FOOTWORK

Proper footwork is the correct movement by the keeper to get to the ball (intercept) or to get in line with the ball (cover the angle) as quickly as possible. Footwork consists of movement in all directions—forward, lateral, and backward. Footwork practice should begin in the warm-up and should be a part of every training exercise.

There's a saying in goalkeeping that "You can't save what your feet can't get you to." Your hands are of no use if your feet don't bring you to where you need to be. And it's the feet that determine whether the keepers can adjust their body in all the various ways required to get to the ball. If the feet don't move properly and don't wind up in the right position, the keeper won't have the balance needed to make the save.

When keepers are having problems with certain saves, the goalkeeper coach should pay close attention to the keepers' footwork.

Quick Shuffle

No matter where the action is on the field, the moment the ball is struck, the keeper must be set—stopped and in the ready position. The keeper can't make a play while racing to a new location.

Goalkeepers who turn and run across the goal get themselves into trouble. This makes it difficult to quickly get back into the ready position, and the keepers are likely to move too fast and take themselves off the best angle for saving the shot.

That's why it's better to shuffle while facing the play. The shuffle should be done with short, quick steps and without clicking the heels (see figure 4.1). Clicking the heels is a big mistake, because at the moment the heels make contact, the keeper doesn't have the optimal shape or balance to take the next steps needed to launch a save movement.

For the shuffle, the emphasis is on short, quick steps that keep you near the ready position.

Figure 4.1　Proper technique for the shuffle step.

The Crossed-Legs Myth

Many coaches instruct their keepers not to cross their legs when moving across the goal. However, the problem with this instruction can be demonstrated by looking at other sports that require quick side-to-side movement.

For example, in baseball, when a shortstop needs to get a ball between third and second base, the player will cross over to make a backhand catch and throw the ball across the diamond. When basketball players are running down the court to defend, they'll cross their legs because this method is faster. The same goes for football players. So I see no logic in telling keepers to never cross their legs.

You could take the world-record holder in the 100-meter dash and beat him in a short race if he were forced to shuffle while you moved by crossing your legs. Moving by crossing the legs is simply quicker.

The keeper should never, however, cross legs during his movements when an opposing player has the ball at his feet. If the shot comes, the keeper won't be in his ready-position stance. With crossed legs, the keeper's ability to react in any direction is limited.

When the ball is being passed—when it's traveling from player to player—keepers can use crossover steps to make up distance with speed. For example, crossover steps are useful when the keeper needs to move across the goalmouth as the opponent switches the point of attack.

But when an opponent settles the ball and might be able to pull the trigger, it's time to quickly get into the ready position. This is easily accomplished. To perform the crossover movement to shift to the left (figure 4.2*a*), for example, you take your right leg and cross it in front of your left, and the next step is your left foot getting into the basic goalkeeper stance (figure 4.2*b*). With every crossover, the next action can transform into the ready position.

Figure 4.2 Proper technique for the crossover step.

The following exercises simulate game situations in which the keeper must move laterally—and quickly—to make saves.

Advanced Footwork Exercises

Three-Goal Service

Setup

Place two cones in a straight line about 8 yards apart. Place two more cones in a line about 5 yards in front of and on the diagonal from the first two cones. Together the four cones should form an inverted U shape and create three goals approximately 6 yards wide—a left goal, a center goal, and a right goal.

The goalkeeper starts behind the two cones that form the goal on the left. Server 1 begins about 6 yards from the left goal, and server 2 begins about 6 yards from the center goal.

Procedure

The goalkeeper comes through the set of cones on the left and saves a ball from server 1. The keeper uses a crossover step to move laterally to save a shot from server 2 in between the center two cones. The keeper then returns to the starting position, and the cycle repeats. After several saves, the goalkeeper and server 1 begin near the goal on the right, and the keeper alternates saving shots from server 1 at the right goal and server 2 at the center goal.

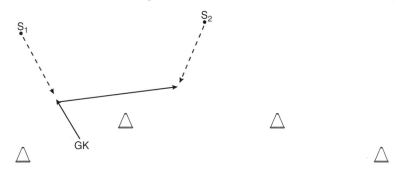

Repetitions

Perform six to ten repetitions on each side.

Variations

Change the service to a drop kick or a ball off the ground. Add in a low ball or a mid-range service.

Near-Post Movement and Handling

Setup

Place two cones in a straight line about 8 yards apart. Place two more cones in a line about 5 yards in front of and on the diagonal from the first two cones. Together the four cones should form an inverted U shape and create three goals approximately 6 yards wide—a left goal, a center goal, and a right goal.

The goalkeeper starts aligned with and centered between the back two cones. The coach stands about 6 to 8 yards in front of the keeper, depending on the type of service. Server 1 begins about 6 yards from the goal on the left, and server 2 begins about 6 yards from the goal on the right.

(continued)

Procedure

The goalkeeper saves a service sent straight up the middle from the coach. Next, the keeper uses a crossover step to move to the goal on the left to save a low or mid-range near-post shot from server 1. The keeper then moves to the opposite side and saves a low or mid-range ball from server 2.

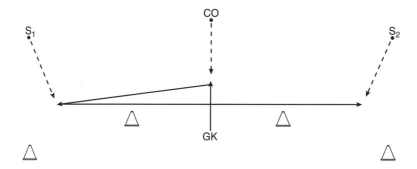

Repetitions

Perform six to ten saves per side.

Variations

Change the type of service to drop kicks and shots off the ground. Make the second service a low or mid-range ball to the near post.

Off the Post II

Setup

Place three cones off both posts diagonally, forming a goal in the middle. The goalkeeper starts at the post, facing out to the field. The server sets up behind the penalty line, near the center of the goal. .

Procedure

The keeper steps over the top of the cones and saves a service from the middle. Next, the keeper goes to the opposite post and performs the same action over the cones. The keeper then saves another service from the middle.

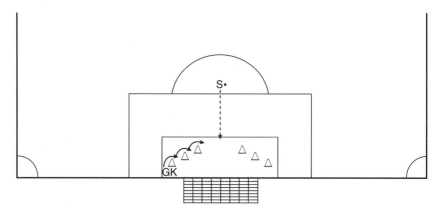

Repetitions

Perform six to ten repetitions.

Variations

Change the service to a drop kick or a shot off the ground. Use this setup to practice low balls and mid-range balls. Have multiple servers in the middle.

Lateral Movement Saves: Footwork

Work half the goal at a time.

Setup

Place three cones laterally across the face of the goal. The first cone should be aligned with the post. The next two cones are about a yard apart. This should nearly split the goal in half. You can use one or two shooters for this exercise.

Procedure

The goalkeeper starts at the first cone and sidesteps over the three cones. After the keeper completes the footwork, server 1, located at the corner of the D, hits a shot between the last cone and the post. The keeper saves the shot.

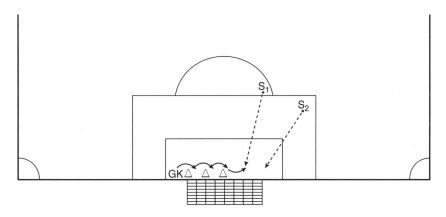

Repetitions

Perform six to eight repetitions on each side.

Variations

Add a second server off the tight angle. This server sends a shot to the near post. To simulate a rebound, have server 2 deliver a low ball to the near post.

Keys to Good Footwork

Coaching Points

- Keepers should move with quick, short steps.
- Using quick shuffles keeps the goalkeeper in the ready position.
- Depending on the distance to be traveled to claim the ball, the keeper may have to use a crossover step. This is only used when the ball is traveling. Keepers should never cross over when the opponent is in contact with the ball (i.e., when he's about to pull the trigger).
- Coaches should check the keeper's body shape and balance.

Common Errors

- Keepers only use shuffle steps to get across the goal. Keepers must be taught to use the crossover step to cover distance quickly.
- The keeper's body shape tends to become erect when moving across the goal. Keepers need to maintain the appropriate shape in order to make the save.
- Keepers run across the goal, losing their shape and angle.

HERE'S THE CATCH

Catching is what really separates goalkeepers from field players. If keepers cannot catch shots sent toward the goal, they are not of much use to the team. All teams *love* keepers with safe hands. At all levels, rebounds lead to goals, so the keeper must develop the ability to hold onto all types of shots.

Catching must be continually trained. It must be a part of every training session at all levels. How the keeper prepares for the catch will usually determine whether the keeper makes a successful grasp. When the keeper catches the ball, her team has possession! Keepers essentially use two types of catches: (1) the "scoop and smother" for balls that arrive below chest level and (2) the two-handed diamond catch for higher balls.

To catch low flying balls, the keeper gets her body behind the ball. The fingers are pointing downward as she scoops the ball into her hands. With the help of the forearms, the keeper embraces the ball, smothering it against the body (see figure 4.3).

A ball that arrives at about chest level or higher requires the keeper to catch the ball with hand contact alone. Thus, the hands move together and form a diamond shape that connects thumb to thumb and index finger to index finger. The diamond creates as much surface area contact with the ball as possible— more than the commonly used W shape, in which only the thumbs connect. The keeper must reach the hands above the ball (see figure 4.4), or at the very least,

Figure 4.3 The *(a)* scoop and *(b)* smother technique for catching low balls.

even with the ball. If the hands make contact underneath the ball, the ball is likely to deflect off the hands and over the keeper. If the keeper's hands are above the ball's center, a deflection will come downward and give the keeper a chance to recover it.

The first step in making the catch is reading the ball's flight to gauge whether it can be scooped and smothered or whether it must be snatched with two hands in the diamond shape. Having made this assessment, the keeper must quickly move into the correct position to make the catch.

Figure 4.4 The diamond method for catching high balls.

MORE THAN AN ATHLETE

From his days as a youth player to his early professional career, Tim Howard was always able to make amazing saves because of his athletic ability. And of all the great keepers the United States has produced, Howard stands out as the best shot stopper. His clean technique and outstanding athleticism are the foundation of his ability as a goalkeeper.

But Howard had to develop into more than just a shot stopper to excel at the game's highest levels. He needed to become a student of the game. Considering the level of competition and opponent that Howard would face in the English Premier League, he knew that relying on pure athletic ability to make saves would not be enough.

So Howard focused intensely on improving his ability to read shooters and to anticipate the actions and movements of the opposition. If Howard isn't seen making as many athletic saves as he did earlier in his career, it's because his positional play has become so good that he's closer to the ball when it flies toward his goal.

Learning to be in the right place at the right time—and having to rely on a diving save less often—comes not just from match experience but also from training. Howard constantly analyzes his play and watches games to better understand where he needs to be in all situations.

Because of his commitment to the tactical aspects of keeper training, Howard became a complete keeper. He still possesses catlike reflexes, great springing ability, and fantastic hands. But the use of his brain is what allows him to play consistently well at the highest levels of the game.

When the U.S. team finished runner-up at the 2009 Confederation Cup (where the team upset defending European champion Spain), Howard won the Golden Glove as the tournament's top keeper. Howard made great saves in the win over Spain in the semifinals and in the final loss to Brazil, but he also continually eliminated goal-scoring chances thanks to his positional play. This combination of great athletic ability and a great sense for the game is why Howard is now considered one of the world's top goalkeepers.

Preparing for the Catch

Catching Balls on the Ground

- The player starts from the ready position.
- The player bends at the waist.
- The palms turn to the ball.
- The hands extend forward.
- The elbows are bent.
- The chest is over the ball.
- The legs are pulled in.
- The body is behind the ball.
- The arms wrap around the ball and pull it into the chest—also called "the bank." The ball is as safe as money in the bank!

Catching flying balls below the waist has the same requirements as the ground ball. Special attention needs to be paid to the distance between the chest and the hands. The keeper must make sure that the ball cannot bounce out of the arms.

Catching Balls in the Air

- The player starts from the ready position.
- The hands move together to make a save.
- The palms face the ball once a shot is taken.
- The hands are *curved*, never flat.
- The hands catch the ball with a large surface area; the fingers are spread around the ball, and the thumbs are behind it. Together, the thumbs and index fingers should form an open diamond shape behind the ball.
- The hands are extended off the body with bent elbows.
- The body is behind the ball.
- The eyes catch the ball! Look the ball into your hands!

Common Errors

1. Keepers have poor initial body shape, especially hand positioning (e.g., the hands are too far apart or too low).
2. Keepers do not focus on the ball all the way into the hands.
3. Keepers' hands are flat when attempting to catch the ball.

Catching Exercises

Double Low Ball

This exercise is excellent for helping a keeper develop low-ball saving technique and for simulating a situation in which the keeper must react to a second play, such as a rebound shot. To keep the focus on positional play, be sure to conduct the exercises on a field with proper markings for the goal area, the penalty area, and the penalty spot. If the field is not lined, figure out a way to mark it.

Setup

Work in front of the goal with three servers (whose target is half the goal). The goalkeeper starts at the post, facing the corner flag and server 1. Server 1 is on the end line. Server 2 is at the corner of the goal area. Server 3 is outside the penalty area and roughly aligned with the post.

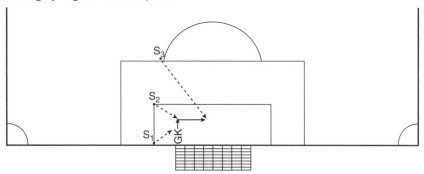

Procedure

Server 1 serves a low ball to the keeper. The keeper "collapses" quickly to save the low ball and gets back on his feet as fast as possible. The keeper then saves a low ball from server 2. The keeper gets up immediately, finds server 3, and saves server 3's shot from the top of the penalty area on the same side of the goal. Repeat the sequence.

Repetitions

Perform four to six repetitions of the sequence.

Variation

Have servers 1 and 2 deliver mid-range balls.

Perfect 30

This exercise is a great way to end a practice session. I particularly like to use this exercise the day before a match to give the keeper confidence. Strive for clean catches throughout and be sure to finish each set with a clean catch.

Setup

The keeper sets up in goal. The coach stands 6 to 8 yards away.

Procedure

The goalkeeper saves 10 volleys from the coach. The keeper then saves 10 drop kicks from the coach. Next, the keeper starts with the ball and rolls it to the coach, who hits a first-time ball back to the keeper's hands (ten repetitions).

PLAYING THE ANGLES

The purpose of angle play is to make the goal as small as possible for the shooter. By leaving his goal line in the direction of the shooter, the goalkeeper can decrease the area available for the attacker to shoot at.

Good angle play makes the life of the keeper much easier. It forces shooters to shoot too wide or too high. The best keepers save shots without ever touching the ball. Their angle approach forces the shooter into a difficult shot or forces him to miss the goal. When a goalkeeper is in the perfect position, the keeper can reach the shot without diving.

The goalkeeper has a good deal of area to cover: near post (figure 4.5), far post (figure 4.6), and crossbar (figure 4.7). But there's always one spot where the keeper is in an optimal position to defend shots that could come to her left, right or high. With alert reading of the attacker's approach and quick movements, the keeper can find the spot.

With proper angle play, keepers avoid unnecessary falling and diving. This prevents injuries and prolongs a keeper's career. Dino Zoff won the 1982 World Cup as Italy's number one keeper at the age of 40. Kasey Keller and Brad Friedel

Figure 4.5 Defending the near post.

Figure 4.6 Defending the far post.

Figure 4.7 Defending the crossbar.

continued to play at a high level in their late 30s and early 40s thanks to great angle play. Tim Howard, the most athletic keeper in U.S. soccer history, turned into an exceptional positional keeper, which led to great success in the English Premier League and with the U.S. national team. He can make the spectacular diving save when he needs to, but he is usually positioned so well that he doesn't have to.

Keepers develop this keen positional sense through experience and proper training. As keepers advance in their levels of competition, their positional play becomes more important. Higher-level field players have better control of where they want to put the ball, so if the keeper is out of position, he is forced into a more difficult save or is punished with a goal.

Goalkeepers' physical qualities also affect their angle play. Taller keepers can be more aggressive and play higher off their line. They can do this because their size covers more of the goal. Keepers with less height or athleticism have to be more conservative so that they can cover all three paths that the ball can take to the net—to both sides of them and over their head. If a shorter keeper plays too far from the goal line, the shooter will be able to beat the keeper over his head.

Tips for Angle Play

1. Keepers should split the center of their body with the center of the ball.
2. Keepers must defend three angles: near post, far post, and crossbar.
3. Overcompensating for any of these angles will leave the keeper vulnerable at the other angles.
4. Keepers should use quick, short steps to move into the proper angle. Large steps will leave the keeper off balance.
5. For every ball touch by the shooter to a particular side, the keeper should move a half step. Full steps will take the keeper off his angle.
6. The coach should always correct improper angle play in ALL exercises.
7. Angle play should be a part of all shot-stopping exercises that the keepers do in training.
8. The coach should stand behind the keeper when addressing angle play. This allows the coach to see the same picture as the keeper.

For exercises designed to train positioning (cutting the angle) and to develop various shot-stopping techniques, accurate service is essential. Servers should vary their delivery, and they should include volleys, drop kicks, and low shots from the ground. Goalkeepers should be coached not to leave rebounds within the frame of the goal. Use a goal, but never train the full length of the goal. Use half the goal as the servers' target.

Angle Play Exercises

Quick Saves

Setup

The keeper sets up in one half of the goal. Server 1 stands to the side of the goal, just outside the 6-yard goal area; server 2 stands near the corner of the penalty area.

Procedure

Server 1 delivers a ball to the goalkeeper at the post. The keeper returns the ball to server 1 and quickly finds server 2. The keeper then cuts the angle and saves server 2's shot.

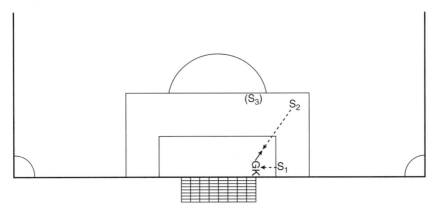

Repetitions

Perform four to six repetitions, then repeat in the other half of the goal.

Variations

Have servers vary the position of the shots (staying within half of the goal). Add a third server; this server begins a few yards to the goal side of server 2. Start with the type of shot (low or mid-range shot) you want to emphasize.

High to Low

Coaching point: Remember that it is OK for the keeper to fall backward while saving at the near post as long as the goalkeeper is in front of the post to push rebounds out of bounds.

Setup

Perform this exercise at a goal with a properly marked goal and penalty area. The goalkeeper starts in the middle of the goal. Server 1 starts in front of the keeper, about 8 yards away. Server 2 stands a few yards behind the corner of the D (where the penalty arc meets the penalty area). Server 3 stands near the corner of the penalty area.

Procedure

The goalkeeper saves a volley from server 1. Next, the keeper moves down the line to save a shot from server 2. The keeper then moves farther down to the near-post angle to save a shot from server 3.

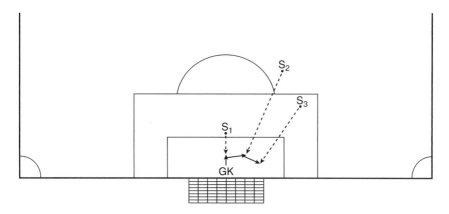

Repetitions

Perform three or four bouts on each side.

Covering All the Angles

A series of shots from different angles helps train positioning. The goalkeeper moves forward and laterally off the goal line to narrow the shooter's angle.

Setup

Seven servers line up in front of the goal in a U shape; servers 1 and 7 are about 2 yards off the corners of the goal area on one side, server 4 is just behind the penalty arc, and the other servers fill the areas in between.

Procedure

The goalkeeper rolls the ball to server 1 and sets his angle. When the goalkeeper is in position to cover the angle properly, the coach signals server 1 to shoot. The keeper rolls the ball to server 2 and gets into position for the next shot. The coach signals server 2 to shoot. Continue the sequence for all seven shooters.

Repetitions

Repeat the sequence as desired.

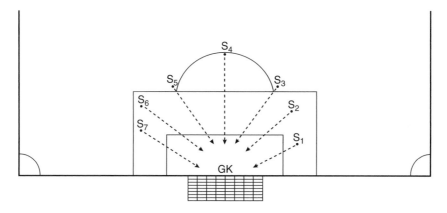

(continued)

Angle Play Exercises *(continued)*

Establishing a High Angle

In this exercise, the keeper works on establishing a high angle off the line to decrease the size of the target.

Setup

Place three cones in a forward line in the middle of the goal. The last cone should be 5 yards off the goal line. The server is positioned at the corner of the D (where the penalty arc meets the penalty area).

Procedure

The goalkeeper starts on the opposite side of the goal from server 1. The keeper uses short shuffle steps to move through the three cones. After the last cone, the keeper moves in line to save a shot from the server.

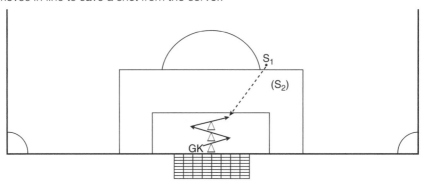

Repetitions

Perform six to eight repetitions on each side.

Variations

Add a second shooter at the tight angle. To simulate a rebound, have the second server serve a low ball to the near post.

PREPARING FOR THE COUNTERATTACK

Figure 4.8 A sprinter's position.

When the opponent is honing in on the goal, the goalkeeper continually adjusts his position to narrow the angle on a potential shot. But what should the keeper be doing when the keeper's team has the ball at the other end?

There may be no danger of an immediate shot, but especially at the higher levels of the game, a counterattack can be launched with lightning speed. In situations such as a corner kick, the keeper's central defenders may be at the other end hoping to head one in. A quick counterattack can be launched with a long pass played behind the defense.

So when the ball is in the opponents' half of the field, the keeper needs to be at the top of the penalty area in a sprinter's position, ready to run out and intercept a pass (see figure 4.8).

COUNTERINTELLIGENCE: "BIG" KEEPERS *ARE* DIFFICULT TO BEAT

Taylor Twellman is not a player whom Major League Soccer goalkeepers enjoy seeing on the field. The Missouri product, who played college ball at the University of Maryland, scored more than 100 MLS goals during his first eight seasons in the league.

Hard, accurate shots—pulling the trigger with little indication of which corner he's aiming for—have been the key to his success. Twellman denies that there is any deep secret to his approach. "When I've got a shot, I strike," he says. "Usually I hit it low and hard."

According to Twellman, the goalkeepers who present problems are those who "make themselves big. When, right before you strike the ball, you see the keeper in your peripheral vision, it can throw you off. It can make the shooter second-guess himself in the last split second, and the shot goes wide or high."

Keepers "make themselves big" with good positioning. The keeper who moves off his line—a few feet or a few yards, depending on where the shooter is—cuts down the angle and puts himself in the shooter's line of sight.

Early in his career, goalkeeper Tony Meola would use practice time to experiment with his positioning. By doing this, he'd sometimes get beaten in practice, but it taught him to gauge how far off his line he should come. "I constantly tested my range and my starting position," says Meola.

PREVENTING SHAPE SHIFTING

It's the goalkeeper coach's job to spot errors in body shape and to train keepers to correct those errors. As with many things, repetition leads to perfection, and young keepers will comprehend how important body shape is as they experience success when they start from the correct position. Once they get used to the right shape and begin taking it whenever they're protecting the goal, goalkeepers see how easy the saves become. Catching, falling, diving, and sprinting off the line to collect a through ball (penetrating pass) all become less difficult. Having achieved good results, keepers are motivated to continue to use that body shape.

Goalkeepers generally establish their set position when they are in their teens. If I looked at tape of when I coached Timmy Howard at age 12, I'm sure I'd see that his shape is somewhat different than at 30 years old. As a young player matures and gains experience, he learns what works best for him. Gains in size and strength may lead a keeper to make slight adjustments in alignment or degree of flexion.

By the time keepers are 18 or 19, when they're done growing, they pretty much have it down. They know how to maximize their athleticism through their shape. Still, making sure a keeper's body is in the right shape is a never-ending process. When an experienced keeper gives up a soft goal, there's a good chance the error can be traced back to bad body shape. The keeper coach and the keeper must monitor body shape on a regular basis.

Diving Saves:
To Fly and Land Safely

Perhaps the only play in soccer that produces more cheers than a goal scored is the diving save. Goalkeepers perform other crucial tasks, such as pulling down a threatening cross amid a crowd of jostling players, but flying through the air to stop a shot is one of the most spectacular feats in all of sports. In addition to the strength and power required to pull off the diving save, it is the grace and agility displayed by the keeper that make the maneuver a wonderful thing to watch. And it's often a game saver!

Goalkeepers dream about making diving saves. Flying through the air to make a save on a ball ticketed for the upper corner is what keepers live for. Hearing the roar of the crowd as the keeper robs the opponent of a certain goal makes all the hard training worthwhile.

Although keepers love the diving save, it is a very difficult technical task. It is also used sparingly in the practical world of goalkeeping. And training this technical skill is unique.

The more diving they do in training, the more likely goalkeepers are to suffer injuries. And coaches must be careful not to turn their keepers into *flyers*—our term for keepers who dive for every ball whether it's necessary or not. Young keepers often do this because they believe that diving is the essence of goalkeeping. The result is that many "soft" goals are given up because the keeper is embellishing the appropriate actions and not using proper and practical goalkeeping procedures.

Thus, coaches should introduce diving with progression training. They must teach proper technique and must be prudent about how much training time is dedicated to diving practice.

Goalkeepers should strive to use their game-reading skills and positioning acumen to reach balls without having to dive whenever possible. But the soccer goal is 8 feet (2.5 m) high and 8 yards wide. That gives the shooter 192 square feet (58 square m) of area to aim at; therefore, goalkeepers need to perfect the art of flying for the ball when necessary. The ability to make these diving saves is part of the athleticism that all keepers must possess to play the position.

One reason young players are attracted to the goalkeeper position is that they want to fly around. They're eager to make the diving save. But when is a player ready to dive? Youngsters will be able to dive when they're physically strong enough. If a 9- or 10-year-old is comfortable diving and knows how to land safely, that's great. Most keepers are ready to learn the skill by the time they are in their early teens. When the keeper is physically ready to dive and has mastered the nondiving save, the coach should introduce diving by first focusing on falling. Diving is basically falling, except you take to the air.

GETTING READY FOR TAKEOFF

Always find a soft patch of grass or sand for diving practice. Sand is excellent for several reasons. It provides a safe landing for the keepers. This will help older keepers avoid injury, and it will give young keepers confidence. Also, driving out of the sand to make a diving save will help keepers develop leg strength and power.

The coach must make sure that all the mechanics that lead into the dive are solid. Each activity builds on the previous one. The order of progression is as follows:

1. Body shape
2. Footwork
3. Catching
4. Falling
5. Diving

At the end of this progression, the keepers get to make diving saves, which is what they all want to do. Diving correctly and avoiding injury are the most important things when learning the skill.

LEARNING TO FALL

You want to first make sure that the keepers' falling technique is solid. Then their strength, power, and confidence will get them into the diving portion.

When coaching diving, be sure that everything is controlled and that the training is set up for success so that the keeper isn't exposed to injury. Don't blast the ball in the corner of the net and tell the keeper to fling his body at it. Instead, take a step-by-step approach.

To teach falling, start the keepers in a seated position, and work your way up. Novice divers must learn to use the ball as a cushion to soften the fall. Make sure that they're not landing on their elbow or shoulder, because that can lead to serious injuries.

A flying keeper who is careless or who uses improper technique can dislocate an elbow or break a collarbone. I've seen a whole host of such injuries over the years, and they are not pretty. So you need to make sure that all the instructions and precautions are taken care of before you get the kids flying around.

PROGRESS SLOWLY INTO THE FULL DIVE

Teach keepers to dive at a young age so they can make mistakes and not hurt themselves. Start with the keeper close to the ground, preferably in a baseball catcher's position. This will give the keepers confidence that they can get off the ground and land without getting hurt. Psychologically, this method is better because the keepers don't fear diving a long way. They need to progress slowly into a full dive. Once the keepers are comfortable diving out of the catcher's position to both sides, you can move them into a standing position. The coach should serve a ball that makes the keeper dive but not at a full stretch. The exercise progression provided later in this chapter can be used as an introduction to diving or as a means of brushing up on diving technique.

For better control and placement, the best method for serving balls is out of the hand. Good placement on the serve allows the keeper to be confident and not worry about injury. At full stretch, the keeper becomes susceptible to injury. If a young keeper gets hurt diving, it will take some time to get her comfortable again in the activity.

Once the keeper is comfortable diving from a standing position, it's time to add the footwork component. No matter how big a keeper is, she will not be able to cover the entire goal just by diving. The footwork mechanics used to save low balls and mid-range balls should be applied here as well.

The keeper needs to use footwork to get close enough to the shot so she can dive to make a save. The step with the leg closest to the ball is called the power step. The keeper needs to push off that leg and drive the hips through the ball. Thinking in this manner will propel the keeper through the goal and allow her to either catch the shot or get a solid hand on it and push it away.

Andy Mead/Icon SMI

Tim Howard flies high to save a shot for Manchester United.

THE RIGHT EQUIPMENT

During training, goalkeepers should be dressed for maximum protection: long pants, long sleeves, and shin guards. I prefer that keepers always wear shin guards at practice, not only to protect them from injury, but also because they have to wear them in games and should be used to them.

Long pants are especially important at the lower levels of competition, where practice fields can be hard and rocky. There's no reason to risk scratches and scrapes that can be prevented by covering up the skin. During games, keepers can wear shorts if that's what they're most comfortable in. But if the game is on artificial turf, the keeper should use long pants.

Some goalkeeper jerseys and pants come with padding. These may be good options if the padding does not constrict movement and if the keeper feels comfortable wearing them. Fortunately, the technology has advanced in recent years, and padded wear (e.g., elbow and hip protection) isn't as bulky as it used to be.

For the most part, any equipment that prevents injury and doesn't impede a keeper's movement is beneficial. You can let a young keeper wear elbow pads at practice if it makes her feel more confident. However, knee pads really don't offer much protection. In addition, allowing keepers to wear knee pads can send the message that it's OK to fall on the knees, encouraging a technique that is not only improper but may also lead to injury.

Keeper gloves are a necessity, and various types are available. In general, keepers should look for gloves that help kill the pace of a hard-hit stinging ball without giving up mobility. The modern foam palm provides shock absorption without causing the keeper to lose a feel for the ball. How thick a glove the keeper wants is a matter of personal preference. The average youth keeper will probably be fine in a relatively thin glove. Goalkeepers often switch to thicker gloves when they reach the highest levels, where shots fly much faster.

A club or a keeper coach may have various types of gloves that keepers can try out. At a store, keepers should try out the various gloves and have someone toss some balls to them—while doing as little damage to the shop as possible!

After determining how thick a padding you like in the palm, what matters most is the right fit. The gloves shouldn't be too tight. Fingers in a glove, like toes in a shoe, need a little bit of wiggle room in front. But there shouldn't be too much room between the fingertips and the end of the glove. The extra material gets in the way and can impede the keeper's ability to get a good grip on the ball. If there's so much extra fabric that it can be bent back or folded over, this indicates that the glove is too big.

The choice of what kind of cleats to wear depends in large part on the playing surface. For higher-level keepers who play on nice grass, screw-in cleats are the best option. Goalkeepers cannot afford to slip when they take those few crucial steps before getting to the ball. Because keepers don't have to run all over the field, they can afford to wear screw-in studs even when the field isn't perfectly soft. And they need the extra grip that the screw-in studs offer. Younger keepers, who often play on fields that are harder than elite-level fields, will usually find that molded cleats suffice. But they should never wear flats or artificial turf shoes when playing on real grass because this will result in a loss of traction. Without good traction, the keeper won't be able to dig in and get a good push toward the ball. The keeper will also have difficulty trying to explode off the line or change direction quickly and jump.

Because teams play on various fields throughout the season, a keeper may want to own more than one set of soccer shoes: molded for hard grass, screw-ins for softer fields, and artificial turf shoes. (Molded cleats can work well on modern artificial fields, which have more give than the older synthetic turf fields that were more like carpets than grass.)

The bottom line is that keepers can't risk slipping or falling. I always have my players come to the field early so they can test their cleats on the game field before the warm-up. This gives them plenty of time to change into the best shoes.

When the glare of the sun is an issue, keepers should feel free to wear a baseball-style cap. A visor is fine if that's what the keeper prefers, but caps tend to be more stable, and most keepers think they look better. If keepers like eye black—the grease that football players often smear under their eyes to reduce glare from the sun or floodlights—they should feel free to use it. The effectiveness of eye black and antiglare patches is debatable. But if either product feels right to the keeper, he should go for it.

Most stadiums are laid out so that the sun is not an issue, which is why we rarely see pro keepers wearing caps anymore. But keepers may want to keep a cap in their equipment bag just in case.

To get close to the shot, the keeper must take a straight path to the ball. The shortest distance between two points is a straight line, so that is how the keeper should travel. If the keeper arches or dives over the ball, the ball can go underneath the keeper's body.

Some coaches have players dive over an obstacle before getting to the tossed ball. The keeper leaps over cones, small hurdles, or a rope. But I believe that early on the goalkeepers should be allowed to decide how high they're going to go. And I don't want them diving high for a ball that's lower than the rope. I'd rather have them dive for the ball without any obstacles. That way, they get into the habit of going directly to the ball, as opposed to diving over something.

For older, more experienced goalkeepers, diving over barriers helps train leaping ability. Hurdles and flags with string hung across them work well. The key is to make sure that the service is appropriate to the height of the barrier. And the barrier needs to be set at a realistic height. For example, we would not have a goalkeeper dive over a hurdle to save a low ball. The keeper dives over these barriers to save balls that are hit at the appropriate height. That is why serving out of the hand may be best for diving exercises.

PRUDENT PRACTICE

Make sure keepers do not overtrain when working on diving. This kind of practice takes a great toll on the keeper's body, regardless of age. Coaches need to have a good feel for their keepers' physical well-being when training.

I believe that players at the highest level of soccer should never do a training session on just diving. Why? These are professional keepers who have made diving saves over the years. They will play in a 10-month season that includes training a minimum of five days a week. Having them fly around in training will only hurt their body. It makes them sore and heavy legged—this is not how you want your keepers to feel during a long season. The senior keepers will get enough opportunities in a normal training session to make diving saves.

Even young keepers need limited training on just diving. Once the keepers learn the technique, a training session solely on diving is rarely needed. Any exercise that involves shooting—either by the keeper coach or the team—will automatically have a diving component. Also, if young keepers begin to fly around to make saves, they will not learn to read shooters or to establish proper angle play, which is paramount to being a top-flight keeper.

Thus, when you do need a session with a young keeper on diving, the repetitions should be short (four to six), and the session should not last long. Keepers shouldn't make more than four to six dives on each side. You don't want your keepers ending up with black-and-blue hips. Keepers in their midteens only need a diving session once every two weeks. They will be diving during other parts of practice, such as in the small-sided games and scrimmages. And remember that all mid-range exercises can become diving exercises by changing the height of the service and the distance that the serve is placed away from the keeper.

DIVING TECHNIQUE

No matter where the ball is headed, the proper technique for a diving save will include some basic procedures. These tried-and-true steps for keepers offer the best chance to make the save.

The keeper should always start in the proper ready position. The weight is on the balls of the feet, the knees are slightly bent, the upper body is leaning slightly forward, and the hands and head are in place. In this position, the keeper is poised for action.

The shoulders should stay square to the field regardless of which side the ball has been hit to so that the keeper is in position to land on the side. Rotating the shoulders over will result in a "Superman" dive, which covers less of the goal and makes it nearly impossible to catch the ball. The Superman dive sets the keepers up to land on their belly, which increases the risk of rib, collarbone, and wrist injuries.

If the shot is close, the keeper can use a short, quick shuffle step (if needed) to get nearer to the shot before diving. If the shot is headed farther away, the keeper should use a crossover step to get closer to the ball before diving. The goalkeeper should point the near foot—the foot closest to the ball—diagonally at the path of the ball to start the body in a forward motion. The near foot should provide the power to begin traveling to the ball. Depending on the distance, getting to the ball may require short shuffle steps, a crossover step, or a wedge step (a short and quick step in the direction of the ball used for power and explosion). The keeper should push or drive the hips through the shot to help cover the distance and to allow for maximum body mass behind the ball. The keeper must not arch toward or dive over the ball; the upper body should be on a diagonal path straight to the ball and should be relaxed to form a cushion for the ball. The head is held still, and the eyes look through the window created by the arms and hands.

For low saves, once the keeper has traveled the necessary distance to make the save, the keeper begins the fall with a progressive collapsing at the ankle, the side of the calf, the thigh, and the hip. The arms are bent and extended off the body to create a lane for the body to fall on the side. With the palms facing the ball, both hands should move together to the side that the shot is aimed at. This will automatically lower the upper body. Whenever possible, keepers should try to make the save with two hands. If they are forced to use one hand, it should be a stiff hand to push the ball to safety. They must not flick the ball away with the wrist. Especially when balls are hit with pace, flicking the ball increases the chance that the keeper will merely deflect the ball into the goal; a stiff-handed push applies more surface area to the ball and allows greater control. The keeper can use a caught ball as a "third hand" to cushion the fall to the ground.

Getting Down: Saving Low Balls

The most common shot that a goalkeeper faces is the low ball. Keepers need to fall to save the low ball, and the save is best made when the keeper takes a straight line to save the shot. The proper technique for saving a low ball includes these steps:

1. Begin to move in the direction of the ball.
2. Point the toe of the foot nearest the ball diagonally at the path of the ball (figure 5.1*a*).
3. Turn the palms to the ball, and bring the hands to the shot (figure 5.1*b*).
4. Collapse into the fall, beginning with the feet and moving up the body (figure 5.1*c*).
5. Get behind the ball.
6. Make the save off the body and quickly wrap both arms around the ball (figure 5.1*d*).

Figure 5.1 Proper technique for saving low balls.

Saving Balls at Mid-Range Height

Balls flying at mid-range height, around waist level, may require falling or diving. The technique for saving these balls is similar to that for saving low balls:

1. Begin to move the upper body behind and in line with the shot, keeping the shoulders square to the field.
2. Keep the hands off the body and keep the elbows bent while preparing to catch the ball in the soft part of the hands (figure 5.2*a*).
3. Place the *head in line with the shot* to achieve the correct height and body shape to make the save (figure 5.2*b*).
4. Keep the upper body relaxed as the hips push through the shot. Hold the head still and look through the window created by the arms (figure 5.2*c*).
5. Once the ball is caught, bring it down to the ground to cushion the fall while keeping one hand on top of the ball and the other hand behind the ball to retain possession (figure 5.2*d*).

Figure 5.2 Proper technique for saving mid-range balls.

Saving Balls When the Keeper Must Fly

The technique for diving is basically the same as for falling and saving mid-range balls:

1. Use fast, balanced footwork to get into position to save the shot.
2. Keep the shoulders facing the field to avoid landing on the belly (figure 5.3*a*).

3. Use the near leg to take a power step to drive to the ball. Bring the opposite leg up and slightly across the chest for balance (figure 5.3*b*).

4. Use the ball as a "third hand" to cushion the fall while keeping one hand on top of the ball and the other hand behind the ball to retain possession (figure 5.3*c*).

Figure 5.3   Proper technique for diving.

Common Errors

Coaches (or keepers who watch videos of themselves) should look for flaws in the entire process to pinpoint why the keepers aren't making the saves. Common errors include the following:

- The keeper is not using enough or the correct type of footwork to cover the distance to save the shot.
- The keeper is rotating the shoulders to the ball and therefore falling onto the belly.
- The keeper is stepping forward with the near foot, forcing the body to fall backward when making the save.
- The keeper is flying to save a shot hit on the ground and letting the ball sneak underneath the arms. Young keepers often do this to jazz up saves. (Keepers need to remember that the shortest distance between two points is a straight line. They must bring the body directly to the ball.)
- The keeper is holding the upper body stiffly so that the ball rebounds off the body.
- The keeper is failing to look the ball directly into the hands.

Progression Practice for Diving Saves

Keep the repetitions for the exercises in this progression to a minimum.

Exercise 1: From a Sitting Position

This exercise is a building block for saving low balls, saving balls hit in the air around waist height, and diving.

Setup

The keeper sits with heels on the ground, toes up, elbows bent, and arms and hands ready to make a save *(a)*. A ball is placed diagonally off to each side of the keeper.

Procedure

On the coach's command, the keeper pushes the hips to a side, falls to her side, and saves a tossed ball *(b)*. The keeper's hands should be placed so that one is on top of the ball and the other is behind the ball.

Exercise 2: From the Knees

After several repetitions from a seated position, the next step brings the keeper higher.

Setup

The keeper is in a starting position on the knees. The keeper's upper body is bent forward, the arms are off the body, and the elbows are bent.

Procedure

On the coach's command, the keeper collapses to her side *(a)* to save a ball tossed to the side *(b)*. This should be repeated several times to both sides.

Exercise 3: Catcher's Position

This exercise introduces the first phase of the footwork needed to correctly make the diving save. The keeper will also start pushing the hips through the shot. This gives the keeper the power to reach shots with the maximum body mass behind the ball.

Setup

The ball is tossed as in the seated and on-the-knees exercises. The keeper is stationed like a baseball catcher, crouched on bent knees.

Procedure

The coach gives the keeper commands before the keeper moves to the ball. "Set!" means the keeper is ready. "Step!" prompts the keeper to point the near-foot toe diagonally at the direction the ball will come from (a). "Save!" orders the keeper to the ball (b). The upper body falls over to secure the ball in the keeper's hands.

Exercise 4: From the Standing Position

The keeper has progressed through three phases (seated, on knees, and crouched) and now begins on the feet.

Setup

The balls are tossed to the keeper's sides as in the previous exercises. The keeper stands and is in a light bounce known as a training jog.

Procedure

The keeper responds to a series of commands from the coach. At the command of "Training jog," the keeper is primed for the save. At "Set," the keeper's body comes to rest; the feet are set, and the keeper assumes the proper body shape. At "Step," the near-foot toe is pointed diagonally at the direction the ball will come from; the body gets low in the direction of the save, and the hands reach together toward the ball as it is tossed (a). At "Save," the keeper falls and wraps the ball into the hands (b).

WHICH HAND?

When a keeper must make a diving save for a ball hit over her head or shoulder, she is forced to tip the ball away if she cannot catch it. For these saves, the steadfast rule has been that keepers should use their higher hand; that is, if diving to her right to save a high ball, the keeper should use her left hand—the upper one.

For many keepers, this is still the best method for saving that type of shot. However, some athletic keepers can make that save with their bottom hand. For these keepers, using the bottom hand is quicker and provides a straight line to the ball.

When I first started coaching, I too believed that using the top hand was the best way to make a save on a high ball. However, through good fortune, I was able to coach two amazingly athletic keepers in Tim Howard and Kori Hunter. Both possessed great power and explosion (38-inch vertical jumps), so they were capable of getting to those balls with their bottom hand.

While coaching these two goalkeepers, I saw time and time again how much quicker they got to the high shot than keepers who went with their opposite hand. I quickly changed my coaching, not their technique. Their way was most effective. So if you have an athletic keeper who can go with the bottom hand, you should let the keeper do so.

THE MAN IN BLACK

The Russian goalkeeper Lev Yashin, the greatest keeper of the 1950s and 1960s, is credited with revolutionizing the position. While his predecessors and contemporaries carried out their job mainly by staying on their goal line for shot stopping, Yashin took command of the entire penalty area. Patrolling the entire area—always wearing black—he became known as the "Black Panther."

Other innovations that Yashin brought to the position include punching the ball away in difficult situations and sparking counterattacks with a quick throw to teammates. And he was a constant communicator—so much so that his wife, Valentina, suggested that he yelled too much. Yashin explained that from the goal he had the best view and that his teammates encouraged him to advise them throughout the game.

Yashin also reached balls that looked like certain goals. This earned him another nickname: "The Black Spider." During a career that spanned a quarter century, he saved more than 100 penalty kicks. "When Lev Yashin covered the goal, not a pinhole was left open," wrote Uruguayan author Eduardo Galeano in *Soccer in Sun and Shadow* (London: Verso, 1998, page 117).

The following exercises replicate the movements and actions of the keeper in the game; therefore, the exercises will help keepers develop most of the technical skills required for the position.

Technical Skill Exercises

AC Milan: Low to High

In this exercise, the goalkeeper must stop shots, recover quickly, find the second shooter, narrow the angle, read the second shooter's first touch to predict the shot, and make another save. The goalkeeper works from a low angle to a high angle.

Setup

The goalkeeper sets up in half of a regulation goal. One server is on the tight angle in the penalty area; a coach with a supply of balls is located right behind this server. A server is also positioned at the corner of the D.

Procedure

The goalkeeper starts by saving a shot from server 1 on the tight angle. As the goalkeeper makes the save, the coach delivers a ball up to the corner of the D. The keeper then finds server 2, who is taking a touch and preparing to shoot. The keeper saves the shot from server 2, and the sequence starts again.

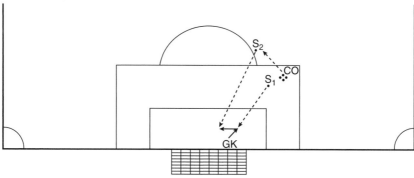

Repetitions

Perform three or four bouts on both sides.

AC Milan: High to Low

Setup

The keeper sets up in the goal. Server 2 is at the corner of the D. A coach with a supply of balls is between them.

Procedure

The goalkeeper starts the exercise by saving a shot from server 1. Right after the goalkeeper saves the shot, the coach delivers a ball to server 2 at the tight angle. The keeper quickly finds server 2 and takes a proper angle. Server 2 takes a touch, and on the second touch, strikes a ball at goal. The keeper saves the shot from server 2, and the sequence starts again with server 1 sending a shot to the goal.

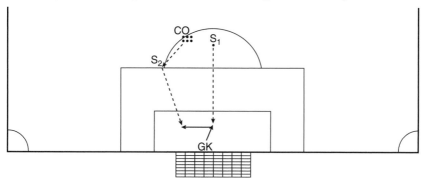

Repetitions

Perform three or four bouts on both sides.

(continued)

Man U: Reading the Shooter

In this exercise, keepers work on angle play, reading shooters after their first touch, footwork, and handling.

Setup

The goalkeeper sets up in the middle of the goal. Server 1 is positioned on the angle to one side of the D. Server 2 is located to the other side of the D. Server 3 is located near the middle of the arc. The coach is at the top of the D with a supply of balls.

Procedure

The coach delivers a ball to server 1, and the goalkeeper slides into position to save a shot from server 1. Server 1 takes a touch and strikes the ball on goal. The keeper saves and returns the ball to the middle. The coach delivers the ball to server 2, and the keeper slides over to save a shot from server 2. The coach rolls a ball back to server 3, who strikes first time on goal, forcing the keeper's quick adjustment to make the save.

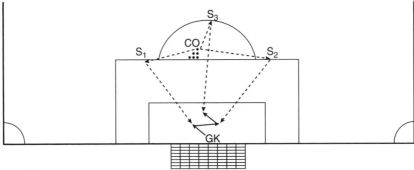

Repetitions

Complete four rounds, changing the starting shot every time.

First-Time Saves

Setup

Server 1 starts with a ball on the end line, and the goalkeeper sets up in one half of the goal, positioned to "square" server 1 (cut off a shooting opportunity). Server 2 begins just outside of the goal area, roughly aligned with the post.

Procedure

Server 1 rolls the ball to server 2, who makes a first-time shot in a location where the goalkeeper must react and move quickly to make the save. The keeper saves the shot from server 2, returns the ball to server 1, and the cycle repeats.

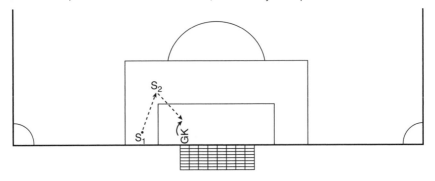

Repetitions

Perform four to six bouts on each side of the goal.

Variations

Server 1 delivers the pass from the corner of the goal area to server 2, who is farther back (at the edge of the penalty area).

Recovery Saves

As a result of a turnover or miscue, the goalkeeper sometimes may not have enough time to get to the ideal angle to make a save. When that happens, the keeper must retreat to the best angle possible, relying on footwork, angle play, proper body shape, and shot-stopping techniques.

Setup

Place three cones 8 to 10 yards from the goal line, spaced evenly across the width of the goal. The goalkeeper starts the exercise at the cone to his left. The server starts a few yards beyond the top of the D with a supply of balls.

Procedure

The server touches the ball forward to strike at goal. At the first touch, the goalkeeper retreats quickly to the middle to establish the best angle he can. The keeper saves the shot, then moves to the cone in the middle. On the touch, again the goalkeeper retreats quickly to save the shot. The keeper then moves to the cone on his right, and the server takes a touch to prepare for the strike. The keeper retreats back to the middle to save the shot. Repeat the sequence moving in the opposite direction.

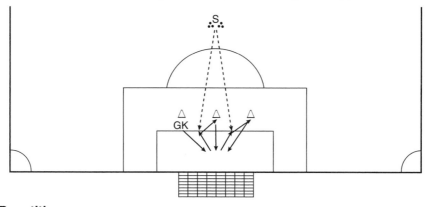

Repetitions

Perform four to six bouts.

Distribution: The Keeper as Orchestrator

Preventing goals may be a goalkeeper's foremost duty, but it's only part of the job. Once the ball is in the goalkeeper's hands or at her feet, the keeper becomes an orchestrator. That's why coaches should stress that goalkeepers are soccer players who happen to have the privilege of using their hands.

Many times during a game, the goalkeeper is the player who initiates her team's attacking approach with her distribution of the ball. The keeper has myriad options for distribution, and to take advantage of all of them, the keeper must master every technique for getting the ball to a teammate.

Goalkeepers must be able to launch an attack with a punt, drop kick, or sidewinder—and they must be able to do so while minimizing risk. They must also be able to throw or roll the ball to their teammate, never failing to reach their target. And they must have the foot skills to effectively deal with teammates' back passes, which they aren't allowed to handle with their hands.

Being good at distributing the ball enables a goalkeeper to help determine the tempo of the game, to give her team an offensive edge, and to make it more difficult for the opponent to launch another attack.

Distribution skills also play a key role in how coaches choose their starting goalkeeper. The keeper who can pass, punt, throw, and roll the ball accurately to teammates will get the nod over the keeper whose distribution enables the opponent to quickly regain possession.

PUNTS, DROP KICKS, AND SIDEWINDERS

Because they can start with the ball in their hands, goalkeepers have more options than field players do for how they can relay the ball to teammates. Three types of kicks start from the hands: punts, drop kicks, and sidewinders. A goalkeeper should be able to master at least two of these three. Preferably, the keeper will master all three! Each type has different technical requirements and is used for various tactics.

IMPROVING THE WEAKER FOOT

Goalkeepers can use the same methods to develop the weaker foot as field players do. Juggling is an effective way to improve the weaker foot. Tapping the ball repeatedly off the foot without letting it hit the ground develops touch and a feel for the ball. Alternating feet is good practice. By trying to get four touches on the left foot while aiming for a total of 10 touches, a right-footed player can effectively train the left foot. The player constantly raises the number of juggles as she improves.

Juggling is one of the great ways for players to improve skills on their own because it trains balance and eye-hand coordination, yet requires only the player and a ball. Even juggling in the living room with a plastic ball or Hacky Sack improves soccer skills.

Passing against the wall with both feet is another training method that players can use on their own. In team situations, players can focus on using the weaker foot in small-sided games. Coaches can organize small-sided games in which goals scored with the weaker foot count double.

Any passing drills that involve using both feet will help improve the weaker foot. As with so many things, it's about repetition.

Punt: Height and Distance

Punting involves striking the ball in the air after dropping it from the hands (figure 6.1). This type of kick enables the keeper to send the ball a long distance upfield and with height.

Keepers should swing through the ball and land on their performing (kicking) foot. The punt is not as accurate as the drop kick or sidewinder. In fact, the punt often results in a 50-50 ball. A punt may even give an edge to the opponent's players because they are facing the ball and can run into it, sending it back the way it came.

Figure 6.1 Proper technique for the punt.

The punt is used when a keeper wants to buy time for his team and gain some territory, especially if his team has been under pressure. Keepers also use this technique if the surface that they are playing on does not allow for a safe drop kick.

Drop Kick: Speed and Accuracy

The drop kick is a half-volley strike. The keeper drops the ball from his hands and makes contact with his foot after the ball has taken a quick, short bounce off the ground (figure 6.2). The drop kick is a more accurate way for the keeper to advance the ball up the field than the punt.

Precise drop kicks enable teams to launch quick counterattacks. They are valuable offensive weapons when the keeper quickly and accurately gets the ball to a teammate before the opposition has time to recover and organize their defense.

Figure 6.2   Proper technique for the drop kick.

Sidewinder: Deadly Counterattack

The sidewinder kick is the most difficult of the three techniques but can be the most effective. The sidewinder requires the keeper to perform a side volley to distribute the ball to a teammate. The keeper throws the ball slightly to the side, turns his body to that side, and brings his hips in line with the height of the ball as he strikes it (figure 6.3).

Figure 6.3   Proper technique for the sidewinder.

Optimally, the ball rockets toward a teammate at about hip height. When done properly, the sidewinder drive sends the ball upfield much faster than a ball on the ground and more accurately than a punt. The sidewinder drive is also easier for a teammate to control or to run on to than a lobbed pass. The sidewinder is the most difficult distribution method to master, but it is well worth the effort.

The sidewinder has been made popular in Central and South America, but keepers all over the world are realizing just how effective this form of distribution can be because it's an excellent method for launching a counterattack. The sidewinder can send the ball into the path of a player sprinting upfield. A toss or a punt, on the other hand, gives opponents much more time to track back and defend. The sidewinder also provides an element of surprise if the keeper unleashes it quickly.

Teams will often keep a fast player forward so that once the keeper catches the ball, the keeper can launch a deadly counterattack with this technique. When done right, the sidewinder is also extremely accurate and allows teams to keep possession higher up the field. Keepers who perfect sidewinders become a valuable part of a team's attacking arsenal.

TONY MEOLA: A MASTER WITH HIS FEET

Tony Meola is a veteran of three World Cups, has won an NCAA title, and is considered one of the best MLS keepers ever. He achieved these things in no small part thanks to his foot skills, which were some of the best ever demonstrated by a keeper.

Meola could hit punts, drop kicks, sidewinders, goal kicks, and back passes with either foot. He could hit them for distance or for possession. Whatever the situation called for, Meola could produce it. He created scoring opportunities for our Kansas City Wizards' team with his distribution. He was truly an extra attacking player.

Teams had to keep players back to defend because of Meola's ability to deliver a drop kick on point to start a counter. He put teams in immediate danger with quick striking distribution.

How did he develop such great feet? One factor was hard work and practice. Meola took great pride in being able to play balls with his feet. He wanted his teammates to be able to play balls back to him so he could initiate an attack.

Another reason for his great feet was that Meola played as a forward in high school. There is no doubt that his unique ability was fostered by playing as a field player. With this in mind, coaches should make sure that their keepers partake in technical sessions with field players and even play in the field some during training. Young keepers should also be given playing time as field players in games.

FROM THE HANDS

The biggest advantage that goalkeepers have over field players is their ability to use their hands. They must exploit this advantage!

One of the biggest flaws of many goalkeepers is poor distribution from their hands. They are careless with their technique or reckless with their decisions when the ball is in their hands. When throwing the ball, keepers should be able to precisely deliver the ball to a teammate. If keepers have a lack of concentration when performing this skill, they deny their team a significant weapon.

Whenever a goalkeeper gives up possession with a throw, it's time to work intensely on that skill. The keeper should *never* lose possession when throwing the ball. A throw from the goalkeeper must be at the proper pace and height to allow the receiver quick and easy control of the ball.

Rolling the Ball

Rolling the ball is the perfect method for getting the ball to a nearby teammate. The keeper bends to roll an easy-to-control ball with the proper pace and *without* a bounce (figure 6.4). Although this is not a difficult maneuver, care should be taken. Goalkeepers can become lazy or careless, and they may roll a ball out with bounce. The ball then becomes difficult for the receiving player to control.

Figure 6.4 Proper technique for rolling the ball.

The primary objective of rolling a ball out is to retain possession. Usually the keeper gives the ball to one of the defenders. The keeper needs to make sure that the player receiving the ball is not under pressure.

Tossing the Ball

A goalkeeper who has mastered throwing the ball can use the toss over any distance. The technique has three steps:

1. Cup the ball between the hand and forearm (figure 6.5*a*).
2. Bring the ball back and to the side of the hip (figure 6.5*b*).
3. Sling the ball over the top of the shoulder (figure 6.5*c*).

Figure 6.5 Proper technique for tossing the ball.

Keepers should throw the ball so that it is easily controlled by the player receiving it. This may require throwing the ball directly to the player's feet or chest. The ball needs to arrive with the proper pace to make it easier for the keeper's teammate to gain control. This throw is also used to initiate counterattacks.

Goalkeepers must be familiar with the skill level of their teammates, recognizing which ones can handle a sharply thrown ball and which ones will falter. They must also know which players can handle a ball thrown at chest level and which ones require a toss at the feet.

TACTICAL CONSIDERATIONS

When goalkeepers have the ball, they must quickly decide where on the field to send the ball, which player should receive it, and which method of distribution to use. If the ball is in the goalkeeper's hands, the rules dictate that the keeper has six seconds to release the ball (or give up an indirect free kick). But many factors go into the decision-making process.

The keeper must consider the following factors:

- The positioning of the goalkeeper's team
- The positioning and pressure of the opponent
- The tempo of the game
- The team strategy
- The weather
- The score
- The time left in the game

Goalkeepers can make life easier for themselves and their team by making the proper decisions on distribution. The correct decision can eliminate pressure, start an attack, or slow or quicken the tempo of play. Each situation is unique, but becoming familiar with the considerations that go into making the proper decision can help a keeper to quickly make the right call.

Risk Versus Reward

No matter what form of distribution the keeper wants to use, the first and most important question to consider is this: Is the risk of this decision worth the reward? There can be *no risk* in the final third of the field at the keeper's end. Keepers who make poor decisions this close to their goal are ultimately punished by giving up goals. The answers to other questions that a keeper must answer are less cut and dried. On balls passed back to the keeper, the keeper must decide whether it's better to try to keep possession or to hit the ball up the field. Is it more beneficial to the team to play the ball wide or to play it to a player in the middle of the field? These tactical decisions need to be made quickly by the keeper based on the strengths and weaknesses of the team, its preferred style of play, and the particular circumstances.

Direct Play

Keepers may choose to play balls far up the field as a tactic designed to minimize the pressure on their team. For example, the team's defenders may not be good on the ball, so playing it to them is not worth the risk. Therefore, the keeper will elect to send the ball far up the field. When the field players don't have the skills required to build the game from the back, the best tactic is usually "direct play" rather than a possession game that moves the ball up the field with passes.

Even when the defensive players are skilled enough to work the ball up the field without coughing it up, the keeper may sometimes opt for the long-distance option to initiate a counterattack. If a ball is passed back and the keeper is under immediate danger or pressure, he should use any of the techniques to hit the ball high, far, and wide if possible.

Top-class keepers can still be accurate and keep possession for their team even when under pressure. They find a favorable player matchup—a teammate who is likely to win an aerial battle, for example—and attempt to play balls to that player. The balls can be played to the head for a flick-on, to the chest for control, or to the ground just in front of the attacker, keeping the defender behind him. With the exception of rolling a ball, any other type of keeper distribution can be direct (i.e., far upfield).

Indirect Play

Certain countries are known for having teams that use a patient buildup out of the back. Brazil, Argentina, and Spain are examples of teams that like to move the ball out of the back by stringing passes together. They send short passes from the back through the midfield and into the attack.

Keepers on teams that favor this strategy need to understand that their team wants them to play balls out for possession. This means the keepers need to throw or pass balls to defenders or midfielders. They need to be very good at playing back passes for possession because their team will often use them to help build out of the back.

Keepers on these teams are also required to change the point of attack when receiving balls. Defenders and midfielders on these teams are usually very comfortable on the ball. They can protect the ball and maintain possession when getting some pressure from an opponent.

Still, the keepers must be careful not to force distribution intended to keep possession when it is too risky. Keepers often feel pressure from their team to help keep possession, and ultimately they make a poor decision and lose possession for their team. This puts immediate pressure on the defense because they are spread wide in the attack.

The Score Matters

The score and time of the match will also influence the decisions that keepers make regarding their method of distribution. Teams may vary in how they choose to address each situation.

FABIEN BARTHEZ: THE GREAT ASSIST

French goalkeeper Fabien Barthez's fabulous foot skills didn't always please his coaches, whose nerves were tested whenever the Frenchman wandered out of his penalty area and juked past opponents with tricky moves. But during the 2000 European Championship final, Barthez showed just how valuable his feet were.

© AP Photo/David Vincent

Fabien Barthez set up a goal that led to France's 2000 European Championship title.

By the time France faced Italy for the title in Rotterdam, Barthez was already one of the world's most accomplished and famous keepers. Known for his shiny bald head, which defender Laurent Blanc would kiss for good luck before every game, Barthez helped France win the 1998 World Cup on home soil. In that World Cup, Barthez conceded only two goals in seven games, stopping a penalty shot against Italy in the quarterfinal shootout, and played "better than brilliant," according to teammate Zinedine Zidane, in the 3-0 final win over Brazil.

In the Euro 2000 final, at the 90th-minute mark, Italy held a 1-0 lead. France was given a free kick about 15 yards outside its own penalty area. Barthez stepped up and launched a rocket that flew to just outside the Italian penalty area, where it was met by a glancing header from French forward David Trezeguet. Trezeguet's header relayed the ball into the path of Sylvain Wiltord, who slammed the ball into the net.

Barthez preserved the tie with a foot save off a shot by Alessandro Del Piero during stoppage time to send the game into overtime, during which Trezeguet scored the golden goal to give France the title.

Hold a Lead

When holding a lead in later stages of a match, some teams elect to play long balls forward to relieve pressure and to force the opponent into attacking from its own half. This allows the leading team to keep its shape and to keep numbers back. Keepers on these teams will be required to play long balls forward. They should still try to maintain possession. An opponent cannot score a goal if it does not have the ball.

In fact, focusing mainly on retaining possession is a reasonable tactic for teams holding a lead. The goalkeeper's challenge in this situation is to distribute the ball in a way that will keep possession for the team while minimizing the risk. Keepers must look for the safest distribution possible.

Comeback Time

When behind in the score late in a match, some teams may want to quickly send the ball far up the field to create scoring opportunities. Keepers need to use the appropriate form of distribution to get the ball into the attacking third as quickly as possible.

Other teams may elect to continue playing "their game" and build the ball out of the back even when they are behind. These teams believe that they are more effective in the attack when they work the ball up the field.

Punting the ball far upfield may lead to the fortuitous bounce that creates a scoring chance, or it may make it easier for the opponent to regain possession. As always, keepers must be able to read the game and consider their team's strengths and weaknesses. And they must be in tune with how their team approaches goal-up and goal-down situations.

Tie Score

A tied game can mean many different things. All games start out that way and are tied for much of the time. During these periods, the keeper distributes the ball according to the opportunities that present themselves and the game plan. Late in the match, the strategy will depend on the circumstances. In league play, a team tied on the road may consider that a good result and may play cautiously as if trying to hold onto a lead. But when a tie is an unsatisfactory result, the keeper will approach distribution late in the game as she would if her team were trying to launch a comeback.

Wide Versus Middle

In general, sending the ball wide is less risky, especially if the target is in the keeper's half of the field. If the opponent intercepts the keeper's pass, punt, or throw on the wing, there's more distance to be covered on the way to the goal and a better chance for the defenders to seal the gaps. If the ball is intercepted in the middle, the opponent might have a straight path to the goal.

Also, consider that a pass to a player positioned centrally usually requires the keeper's teammate to control the ball while facing her own goal and forces her to cope with the opposing player's momentum. It can be very difficult to receive and control a ball while facing one's own goal as an opponent runs toward the ball.

In a keeper's own half, distribution to a central player is only safe when the keeper's teammate has put herself into an open space and the keeper can deliver the ball quickly and accurately so that it arrives before the opponent does.

A long punt down the middle into the opponent's half is less perilous simply because the opponent has a longer distance to cover on the counterattack. But even so, a ball won by a central defender down the middle can pose a greater threat than one intercepted by an outside back.

Needless to say, a crucial factor is the ability of the keeper's teammates to win high balls and to control low distribution. But in general, distribution down the middle requires more caution and more skill from the keeper and the receiver.

COPING WITH THE BACK PASS

There was a time when foot skills weren't so crucial for goalkeepers, but since a 1992 rule change, keepers are prohibited from handling the ball when it is passed by a teammate. (A keeper can only handle an intentional pass from a teammate if the ball is headed, chested, or hit with the thigh.) In addition, keepers may not handle a throw-in from a teammate. That means keepers must be able to trap, dribble, and pass while under pressure.

A goalkeeper who can competently trap, dribble, and pass adds an important dimension to his team. When the keeper has these skills, defenders on the team can play the ball back to the keeper instead of hoofing it out of bounds or aimlessly upfield. Goalkeepers with the following characteristics offer their team the option of playing the ball back to them.

1. **Good skill with both feet.** Teammates must be able to play the ball back to the keeper without worrying about which foot to play it to. The side of the keeper that the teammate passes the ball to should be determined by which side is safer, not by which foot the keeper is comfortable with. A one-footed keeper will get himself into trouble, creating scoring chances for the opponents.

   Goalkeepers in today's game must have the ability to play balls with both feet. They must be able to pass for possession, to clear balls up the field, and to start a counterattack. They need to master the punt, drop kick, and sidewinder (side volley).

2. **Reliable inside-of-the-foot pass.** Keepers need to have the ability to pass balls with the inside of both feet. This is paramount to being able to maintain possession out of the back because the strike with the inside of the foot is the most accurate method for delivering passes that cover up to 20 yards. A keeper can train this skill along with field players as they do their technical work.

3. **Reliable first-touch instep pass.** Keepers also need to drive balls on the first touch with their instep. This is generally done when the keeper receives a back pass and is under pressure. The keeper has to release the pressure

by playing a long ball up the field. By striking the ball with the instep, the keeper will give the ball distance and height to escape the pressure. Again, the keeper must be able to perform this action with both feet.

4. **Clean first touch.** Keepers must develop their first touch so that they can receive a ball properly and then make the next pass. This is called two-touch goalkeeping. Keepers may be forced into taking a touch because of a poor back pass from a teammate. The proper first touch will set up the next pass for the keeper.

   A clean first touch can also eliminate pressure from the opponent and help the keeper change the point of attack. Keepers can take an extra touch if they are not faced with immediate pressure. But when under pressure, the keeper's first touch must put the ball in position to strike. The keeper shouldn't trap the ball dead, because this puts the keeper in a vulnerable position, needing a subsequent touch to pass the ball.

5. **Ability to block the ball.** Keepers may have to block a ball to safety. This technique involves striking the ball with the inside of either foot with very little swing of the leg. The keeper uses the pace of the ball to create the momentum to advance the ball up the field. This technique is used when a ball is bouncing to the keeper or when the weather conditions are poor. The blocking technique is not meant to keep possession. It's simply a safe way to deal with a difficult back pass.

The following exercises will help keepers master the ability to deal with the back pass so that they can quickly and efficiently do so in any situation.

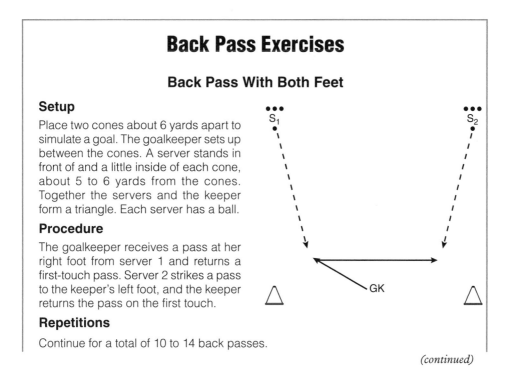

Back Pass Exercises

Back Pass With Both Feet

Setup

Place two cones about 6 yards apart to simulate a goal. The goalkeeper sets up between the cones. A server stands in front of and a little inside of each cone, about 5 to 6 yards from the cones. Together the servers and the keeper form a triangle. Each server has a ball.

Procedure

The goalkeeper receives a pass at her right foot from server 1 and returns a first-touch pass. Server 2 strikes a pass to the keeper's left foot, and the keeper returns the pass on the first touch.

Repetitions

Continue for a total of 10 to 14 back passes.

(continued)

Variations

Have servers deliver balls at a faster pace. The goalkeeper uses two touches to return the ball. If only one server is available, have the server deliver passes to each side of the keeper from a position directly across from the keeper.

Back Pass With Movement

Setup

Place two cones 6 yards apart to simulate a goal. The goalkeeper sets up between the cones. A server stands across from and 5 to 10 yards away from each cone. Each server has a ball.

Procedure

The goalkeeper shuffles over to cone 1 (to his right) and receives a pass from server 1. The keeper returns the ball on the first touch . The keeper then shuffles over to cone 2, receives a pass from server 2, and returns it on the first touch.

Repetitions

Continue for a total of 12 to 14 back passes.

Variations

Have the servers strike the balls for faster pace. The goalkeeper uses two touches to return the ball.

Continuous First-Touch Back Pass

Setup

Place two cones 6 yards apart to simulate a goal. The goalkeeper sets up between the cones. A server stands in front of and a little inside of each cone, about 5 to 6 yards from the cones. Together the servers and the keeper form a triangle. Server 1 begins with a ball.

Procedure

The goalkeeper receives a pass from server 1. The keeper plays a first-touch ball to server 2. Server 2 plays the ball back to the keeper. The keeper plays a first-touch ball to server 1.

Repetitions

Continue for a total of 10 to 14 back passes.

Variations

Have the goalkeeper play two-touch balls back to the servers.

Changing the Point of Attack

This exercise develops the keeper's ability to play a ball out of the back for possession to an outside back or wide midfielder. The keeper receives the ball from one side of the field and plays it out to the other side. This is called changing the point of attack (CPA).

Setup

Server 1 is at the top of the D with a supply of balls. Servers 2 and 3 set up on the opposite side of the field as a back and an outside midfielder. The keeper sets up near the edge of the goal area in front of the server.

Procedure

Server 1 plays a ball into the feet of the goalkeeper. The keeper takes a touch and hits a driven ball out to server 2. Server 1 plays another ball to the keeper, who takes a touch and sends it to server 3.

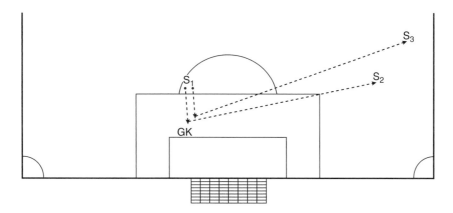

Repetitions

After sending eight balls to the keeper, the servers move to the opposite side of the field and send another eight balls.

Variations

Add additional players (or cones set up as targets). The goalkeeper drives balls to various targets.

Everton Back Pass

This exercise incorporates a shot into back-pass training.

Setup

The goalkeeper sets up off the right post. Use cones or markers, if desired, to set off an area from which the keeper receives and sends balls. Server 1 stands in front of the keeper, about 12 yards away. Server 2 sets up in the penalty arc.

Procedure

Server 1 rolls a pass to the goalkeeper. The keeper receives the ball and takes two touches to play the ball to server 2; the keeper then moves across the goal area to align with server 2. Server 2 controls the ball and shoots on goal. The keeper makes the save and returns the ball to server 1.

(continued)

Everton Back Pass *(continued)*

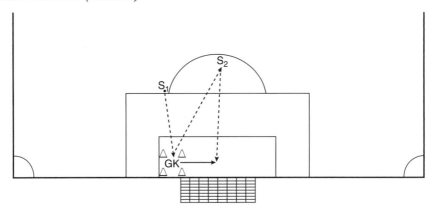

Repetitions

After four to six shots on goal, server 1 and the keeper set up on the other side of the goal, and the sequence is repeated for another four to six shots.

Variations

Have the goalkeeper play the ball on the first touch to server 2. Have server 2 hit first-touch shots.

DETERMINING TEMPO

Keepers can dictate the tempo of the match through their distribution. They can quicken or slow the tempo depending on the game situation and conditions, and they can respond to the momentum shifts that occur during the course of a match. Several scenarios might warrant distribution methods that speed things up. If the opponent is struggling to find its form or is showing signs of fatigue, the keeper may want to keep the pressure on. Or perhaps the opponent prefers to play at a slower pace and gets rattled by quick play. Keepers will want to play at a high tempo when their team is losing a match and time is running out—while avoiding the panic that leads to bad decisions. Teams may prefer to play at a fast tempo if the climate is conducive to it (e.g., in England). And at the pro level, teams playing at home usually want to dictate a fast and aggressive tempo; therefore, the keeper will want to help create that tempo by getting the ball into play quickly.

To up the tempo, the keeper will want to put the ball in play quickly while retaining control. The keeper should also use more long-range methods of delivery. A sidewinder that sends a teammate down the flank or a quick punt to the center forward in the opponent's half will keep things moving. The keeper can also communicate with his teammates that they need to pick up the pace.

Conversely, a team may want to slow the pace of the game for a variety of reasons. If the keeper's teammates are shell-shocked from fending off waves of attacks, the keeper may want to slow things down. When an opponent is firing on all cylinders and a keeper's teammates are gasping for air, the keeper will want to do whatever possible to decrease the pace. In hot weather, a keeper may decide to slow the tempo for obvious reasons. And when his team is holding on to a lead late in games, the keeper should be in *no* hurry to get the ball back into play.

Keepers can delay or slow the game in several fashions. One way is to not pick up the ball immediately with his hands. This will allow the keeper to kill some time before an opponent puts him under pressure. When his team is under great pressure, the keeper may want to take his full six seconds if he has the ball in his hands—or longer if the ball is at his feet—and allow his teammates to catch their breath. Another technique a keeper can use to slow the tempo is to direct the team out to midfield while holding the ball, then drop the ball to the ground and move it out of the penalty area before passing the ball up the field. (Remember, if a goalkeeper has the ball in his hands, drops it, and picks it up again, even if he is still in his penalty area, this is a violation of the rules and earns a dangerous indirect free kick for the opponent.) The keeper might also elect to use safe distribution to the outside backs, giving them a chance to keep possession by stringing passes along the back line before launching an attack.

FIELD AND WEATHER CONDITIONS

When field conditions make it difficult to play a passing game, the keeper will have to adjust her distribution. The keeper will not be able to play out of the back if the field width is tight or if the grass is uneven. In these conditions, the keeper's distribution will become more direct.

Weather conditions can also determine if the keeper should use direct or indirect play. Facing a stiff wind, the keeper may have to play the ball out of the back. Long strikes forward will not be effective into such a wind. On the other hand, a strong wind in favor of the keeper's team may make it beneficial to play long. On a rain-soaked field, the ball is likely to skip farther when it hits the ground, so distribution directly to the feet of a teammate is optimal.

Before the game, the keeper needs to know the coach's strategy for how the ball should be distributed based on the conditions and in general.

chapter 7

Expect the Unexpected: Reading the Game

Many talented goalkeepers—excellent athletes with superb shot-stopping skills—fail to succeed at the higher levels because of their inability to read the game well. This is frustrating to witness, because these players have so many other attributes of great goalkeeping. The tale of such keepers follows a familiar course. Their superb athletic abilities disguise their game-reading deficiency as they climb the ranks of the youth game.

These goalkeepers may get caught out of position but still manage to make a spectacular stop thanks to their athleticism. In fact, they may make more thrilling saves than your average keeper *because* their positioning is so frequently flawed. Because they're rarely getting scored on, they neglect the cerebral requirements of the position, as perhaps do their coaches.

For goalkeepers, reading the game means being able to anticipate the unfolding of an attack so the keeper can get into an optimal position to make a save or cut off a pass. Reading the game and communicating with teammates also enable keepers to organize their defense so that the dangerous scoring opportunities don't develop.

A young keeper may fail to organize his defense on corner kicks or may fail to anticipate the flight of a cross in order to snatch it before it results in a shot. At lower levels, this keeper may still earn his shutouts because he has the athletic ability and reflexes to make the close-range save. But at the higher levels, attackers shoot more accurately, strike with more pace, and are savvy enough to exploit the poor positioning. The keeper who doesn't become an expert at reading the game will eventually suffer.

Proper positioning comes from being able to anticipate how the game develops. To direct their defenders in the proper way to eliminate danger, keepers must comprehend the opponent's attacking trends. For these reasons, coaches must encourage their goalkeepers to be students of the game from a young age. And young keepers must not evaluate their performances merely on shot stopping.

JON BUSCH: MASTER STUDENT

Jon Busch jokes that he's 5-foot-10 "on a good day." That might be average height for an American male, but for a top-level pro goalkeeper like Busch, it's quite a bit on the short side. No matter how tall a goalkeeper is, he must be able to read the game in order to anticipate shots, crosses, and threatening passes—but there's no doubt that Busch's acumen in reading the game has made him one of the top goalkeepers in Major League Soccer.

Bigger keepers can often compensate for a misjudgment because of their reach. This luxury is not an option for Busch. Partly because of this, Busch trained himself to anticipate how an attack will unfold and where he must be when it's time to save the shot, snatch the cross, or intercept the through ball.

"One of the keys for me is that I have always been taught by my coaches, since I was very young, not to just stand there and wait for the shot," says Busch, who played in the 1993 U17 World Cup before a college career that included a final four appearance with UNC Charlotte. He spent more than a decade in the pros, where he earned the 2008 MLS Goalkeeper of the Year honor.

No matter what part of the field the ball is on, Busch follows the play intensely. "You're focusing on how things are developing," he tells us. "You're always thinking about where you're standing and how to adjust as the play unfolds. You're not caught having to backpedal desperately—because you've predicted when the shot will be launched and you're already in the right spot.

"You're not waiting for things to happen. You're totally in tune with the game. When a player comes down the wing, you see his approach and anticipate how he might deliver the cross. You're on your way to the ball as it leaves his foot."

Before a game, Busch does his homework. In addition to watching the video of the next opponent his team will face, he watches additional video of individual opposing players to study their tendencies. He knows which players take corner kicks, free kicks, and penalty kicks and how they tend to send the ball. He notices how and where key attackers look for scoring opportunities. Long before the kickoff, Busch knows which wingers usually send in outswingers and which ones prefer to turn a defender and curve an in-swinger.

Younger keepers may not have access to extensive, detailed video, but they can take advantage of every opportunity to learn about their opponents and the tendencies of those opponents. They can become students of the game who recognize how different types of attackers threaten the goal—and who quickly take appropriate action.

Players of all ages and all sizes can take inspiration from Jon Busch, who proves that game smarts go a long way.

© AP Photo/Steve Milne

Jon Busch more than compensates for his lack of height with his intensity and intelligence.

Reading the game is one of the biggest hurdles facing goalkeepers who strive for greatness, but it is a hurdle that can be cleared when coaches and keepers work together. Experience—both in the goal and on the field—is the best way for goalkeepers to learn to read the game. Studying the play of successful keepers also helps. A keeper coach who can guide the keepers' perception of their own play and that of others can greatly enhance the development of the keepers' skills in this area.

THE COACH ON THE FIELD

The goalkeeper's position on the field provides her with a unique perspective. In fact, the keeper may have the best vantage point for seeing how the opponent's forays unfold and for tracking the field players' positioning. Coaches on the sideline benches don't have as good a view. The goalkeeper is the only one who can truly measure the width at which the field players are positioned.

Goalkeepers must make full use of this advantage. They should attend to all aspects of the game so they can direct their teammates to mark up and cover the gaps. The keepers should also know exactly what the coach's game plan is and should ensure that the players stick to it. By monitoring and assessing the action on the field, keeping the game plan in mind, and communicating intelligently with their teammates, goalkeepers serve as coaches on the field.

THWARTING A STRATEGY

A goalkeeper's ability to read the game will benefit his team in various ways. Let's take a look at one example:

In 2008, the United States faced Argentina at Giants Stadium. Argentina came to New Jersey ranked number one in the world, and a crowd of 78,682 came to see how this team would fare against the Americans. Four days before that game, Argentina had dismantled Mexico, winning 4-1 in San Diego, California. U.S. goalkeeper Tim Howard watched the Argentines' performance against Mexico closely and saw how they had succeeded with crisp combination play through the heart of Los Tricolores' defense.

Howard knew that for the U.S. team to be successful, it had to deny the Argentines their preferred means of attack: the central combinations that create chances inside the penalty area. So Howard played higher off his line and focused on reading the through-ball situations that often sprung free Argentine attackers. Instead of waiting for the shots, Howard disrupted the Argentines before they pulled the trigger on several occasions.

In the first half alone, there were 10 incidents in which Howard picked off a pass, snatched the ball from an Argentine player's feet just as the pass arrived, or was close enough to the attacker to snuff the shot. By playing farther off his line, Howard made it easier for his defenders, because they were able to play higher up. Had he stayed on his goal line, the defenders would have had to defend closer to their own goal and would have been more vulnerable. Instead, the defenders crowded the area in which the Argentines tried to string their passes together.

Howard had read the game and executed properly. As a result, the Argentines changed their approach for the second half, shifting from the central combination play to moving the ball out to the wings and delivering crosses. Howard forced the Argentines to adopt a strategy that they weren't as comfortable with and one that fed into the strengths of the U.S. team; the U.S. central defenders had a size advantage and were adept at winning crosses.

The Americans weren't able to get a goal of their own, but they shut out the best team in the world. The 0-0 tie thrilled the huge crowd at Giants Stadium while giving the Americans a huge boost of confidence before qualifying play began for the 2010 World Cup.

To command the respect and cooperation of the field players, the goalkeeper must have a solid relationship with her teammates, especially the back line and the defensive midfielder (also known as the holding midfielder). The keeper must be able to organize these players and move them around to eliminate goal-scoring chances. The coordination of the field players with each other and with the goalkeeper must become second nature for all parties involved, and that starts on the training ground.

READING AND ORGANIZING IN TRAINING

It's the goalkeeper's job to organize the defenders in the proper way to prevent scoring chances. And practice sessions should be designed to help the keeper and the defenders learn to play together as a unit. Small-group exercises go a long way toward building defensive cohesiveness. These exercises give the keeper a chance to lead the defense, and they give the field players a chance to view the goalkeeper as their leader.

Game Simulation 6v4

This exercise prepares keepers for match action, bringing them in tune with your team's system of play. In this exercise, keepers practice reading the game as well as decision making, organization, shot stopping, and distribution. The field size allows the defenders to push the forwards downfield as they would in a real game. This also creates situations in which the forwards get behind the defense.

Setup

Use one half of a regulation field. Place two small counter goals at the centerline.

Procedure

The keeper works with four backs to defend the regulation goal against six attackers *(a)*. The defending team aims for the two small goals to practice playing out of the back.

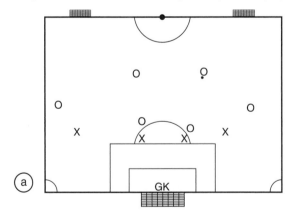

Variations

Have the keeper work with five backs against seven attackers (7v5—see figure *b*).
Have the keeper work with six backs against eight attackers (8v6—see figure *c*).

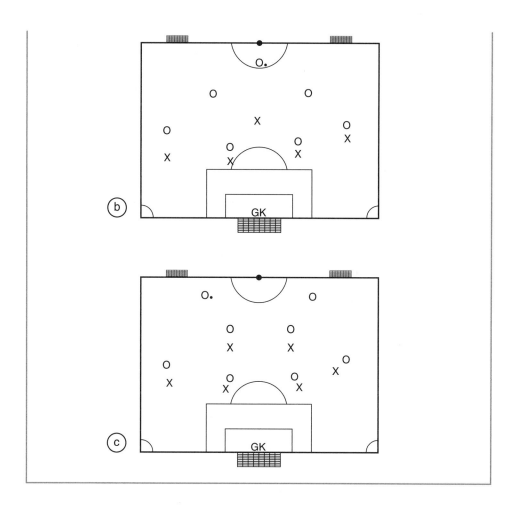

In 2000, when I was the goalkeeper coach for the Kansas City Wizards, we won the MLS title, and keeper Tony Meola won the league MVP honor. The key to our team's success was how well Meola worked together with his defenders. That season, Meola played behind his back four in every small-sided game in practice.

Practices can be easily orchestrated to create the optimal environment for getting players accustomed to playing together. Small-group exercises and game simulations are an excellent way to encourage players to coordinate their play.

Players in small-group games must stay attuned to their roles and responsibilities because the players are coping with wave after wave of attacks. As they play, they're building relationships, increasing their understanding, and synchronizing their movements. Goalkeepers hone their skills in reading the game, and they earn the trust of their teammates.

Allowing keepers to play in the field at practice can also be immensely valuable. It's no surprise that so many great goalkeepers—for example, Tim Howard, Brad Guzan, Brad Friedel, Tony Meola—spent much of their youth soccer playing in the field. Experiencing field-player situations firsthand helps goalkeepers become adept at reading the game.

Playing in the field in small-sided games of 5v2 or 6v3 gives the keeper a chance to think like an attacker. There's nothing like determining where the next pass should go while playing offense to hone a keeper's ability to anticipate potential attacks. Working as a field defender also pays dividends. It gives keepers valuable insight into the quick reactions and proactive plays that defenders are called on to execute in the heat of the game.

COACH'S ROLE

The goalkeeper coach, or the person filling that role, oversees every aspect of the goalkeepers' training. This means running the keeper drills and suggesting strategies as well as overseeing the keepers' interaction with the rest of the team. The more involved the goalkeeper coach is, the better he can guide the goalkeepers' development and nurture their ability to read the game.

Early in the keepers' development, the coach may move the keepers around to the appropriate angles as the play changes directions. For example, some keepers may be hesitant to leave the goal line; the coach will move these keepers a little farther out so that they can intercept a through ball or catch a ball that's hit over their backs' heads. As the keepers progress, the coach can focus the keepers' attention on the finer points of reading the game.

One way a coach can help a keeper anticipate the play is to explain that the keeper is responsible for two-thirds of the field behind the backs. The first third of the area behind the defensive line is too far away for the keeper to cover, but behind that section, the keeper who has the ability to read the play can anticipate through balls and intercept them.

In addition to training the keepers individually, the goalkeeper coach must be a part of functional team training. (If the team doesn't have a keeper coach, then the assistant coach who is responsible for the keepers should be there.) During team training, the keeper coach should help the goalkeepers direct the team, solve problems, and answer questions. The keeper coach should be constantly analyzing plays and evaluating the keepers' positioning and decision making.

The keeper coach will assess, for example, whether the keeper is in the right starting spots when the ball is in certain areas. If the keeper sticks to the line when the action is farther out, he may not be close enough to comprehend the immediate danger. The keeper may be lulled into a false sense of security, and if he doesn't read things quickly, he'll be punished. Alternatively, if the keeper strays too far from the goal, he's vulnerable to a shot chipped over his head and into the goal.

The keeper coach should have the ability to stop training and make corrections when necessary. The coach might offer comments such as the following:

- "Here's where you're in trouble. You need Jackie farther to the right and Sally closer to the penalty spot."
- "Jose should be playing farther out to close off the passing lane down the side."
- "You need to be farther off your line so that you don't give them so much space behind our backs to pass into."

- "You need to be farther out when we've got the ball in their end—this makes it easier to communicate with your teammates. You're a quick keeper; you can move out because you'll be able to recover in time if they launch a long one."

Coaches must be careful not to overdo it or become a distraction by spouting nonstop instructions. Keepers need to learn how to make their own decisions. But when a coach judiciously offers advice and points out positioning flaws, this helps the keepers learn to read the game better. Also, when the field players hear the coach demonstrating the kind of directions to give, those field players will better understand why they're receiving such direction from the keeper.

To test and expand the keepers' ability to assess a situation, the keeper coach should also use questions such as the following:

- "Why do you think that's happening?"
- "Where's a better position for that defender?"

This kind of problem-solving exercise will help build the keepers' confidence.

ORGANIZING THE DEFENSE DURING THE GAME

Soccer is a fluid game in which players on both teams are constantly moving, changing positions, and making off-the-ball runs. From her vantage point in the goal, the keeper can spot attacks on her goal as they begin to take shape. As the "coach on the field," the keeper's job is to organize her own field players to neutralize the threat.

When a left back, for example, begins to make a run into the attack while the ball is on the other side, the keeper can shout out at a midfielder or forward—whose eye is on the ball and not the overlapping left back—to track back.

Also, each time the opponent wins a one-on-one, the keeper must ensure that the shape of the defense adjusts. The immediate danger must be covered without exposing a new, even more dangerous lane of attack for the opponent. For example, if the defensive midfielder gets beat, a central defender must step up to meet the attacker. That leaves the central defender's player unmarked. The keeper may instruct his outside back to tuck in for support (e.g., "Pinch in, John!") because covering the middle is more important at that time than watching the flank. If the ball goes out to the flank, the defenders have a chance of recovering before any damage is done, whereas leaving an unmarked opponent in the middle presents greater danger.

Especially on set plays, the opponents may send extra players in to attack—that is, players who usually stay in their own half. A prime example of this is sending big central defenders up on corner kicks. The keeper must sort out how to cover these intruders, such as calling for his forwards to retreat. The keeper may also notice coverage mismatches. If a small midfielder is marking a tall central back on a corner kick, the keeper may have this midfielder switch marks with a bigger teammate.

Principles of Defense

The goalkeeper must keep the following fundamental principles of defense in mind as she organizes the defense during the game.

- **Put pressure on the ball handler.** An effective defense requires that there's always pressure on the opponent who has the ball. If a single defender is beaten, teammates should be positioned so that they are ready to deny penetration. This requires coordination and balance between the players.

- **Defend from the inside out.** Close down the most dangerous lanes and force the opponent to attack where the defensive team is well-positioned to thwart the foray.

  In most situations, this means directing the play to the outside. When opponents are forced to attack from the flank they have a less direct path to the goal; this allows your central defenders more time to read the approach and often encourages attacking players to launch hopeful, ineffective crosses. Allowing an attack down the middle is more dangerous because it opens up a variety of direct shooting opportunities.

- **Stay compact.** The correct distance between backs to midfielders to forwards is 35 yards from back to front. Players in back and midfield should only have 10 to 12 yards of distance between them.

- **Communicate and Cooperate.** Defenders should track runners off the ball until the keeper or a teammate tells them to release them. To defend combination play, the defender should turn with the runner while a teammate pressures the passer.

- **Be patient.** Don't overcommit and get burned.

- **Focus.** Maintain your concentration and composure.

CONVEYING THE MESSAGE

Keeping in mind the general style of play and specific game plan set by the coach, the goalkeeper reads the game and directs the field players. The field players should expect the goalkeeper to give them instructions and should be ready to follow those instructions. There will be time for discussion afterward, but if the goalkeeper tells players to do something during the game, they should do it.

The keeper's instructions cannot be constant or excessive, though, because the team will stop listening. Think about a boring teacher who drones on and on: The students end up tuning out, and then they miss a crucial instruction when it really matters. The keeper should only talk when it's truly necessary. Even positive remarks should be kept to a minimum. The goalkeeper should not be a cheerleader. Encouragement at certain times is valuable, but constant chatter is not.

The keeper should be confident but not arrogant. At times, the goalkeeper will tell a field player to do something, but the player will not have the time or the ability to do it. There will also be times when the field player is close enough to the situation to see that the keeper's instruction is not the best idea—so the player does something else. As long as it works, that's fine. If it doesn't work, the keeper and the player need to sit down with the coach afterward and figure out why. The goalkeeper needs to have a thick skin because he's not always going to be right.

Sometimes when a keeper calls for the ball and the field player kicks it away, the goalkeeper will look at the field player as if he did something wrong. But the field player may explain, "Hey, the guy was right next to me. He was going to get it before you, so I figured I'd do the safe thing." Fair enough. That's the kind of give-and-take necessary for a healthy working relationship between the keeper and the field players.

The goalkeeper needs to talk to players without berating them. If the keeper makes players feel as if they've made horrible mistakes, they'll start tuning him out. Whether they think the keeper is being unfair or is flat-out wrong, they won't be motivated to listen or to play hard. The keeper needs to talk to players in a way that inspires them to want to work hard. The keeper should be giving consistent, clear, concise information and delivering it in a calm and respectful manner.

FROM START TO FINISH

From the opening play of the game to the final whistle, the goalkeeper is hard at work. During the run of play, players are reacting to runs and movements and to the ball being played from one player to the next. The information communicated by the keeper needs to be especially short and concise. If the goalkeeper overloads the field players with instructions at this time, the players may get confused, and the team might lose its shape.

On dead-ball situations, the defending team does benefit from a short break to organize and mark up. The field players may position themselves properly on their own, but it's the keeper's job to ensure that they eliminate as much danger as possible before the ball is delivered. The goalkeeper may need to maneuver players around or change the matchups. In set-play situations, the goalkeeper is the absolute boss. The keeper should be the only person talking, and any discussion can be done after the play. This guideline needs to be established in training.

Reading the game is a never-ending process. Even after games in which they're hardly called on to make saves and their team wins easily, goalkeepers will still feel exhausted—because they've been concentrating intensely the entire time.

When the keeper's team has the ball, the keeper needs to be focused on the play and thinking about possible developments:

- Are we in danger of losing the ball?
- Are there enough players around the ball to stop a counterattack if the opponents gained possession?

- Could we quickly have the opponent's forwards marked up if the ball changed hands?
- Could we drive a player into the right spot if the ball popped loose?
- Could we get the ball back right away if the opponents stripped it?

OFF-THE-FIELD TRAINING

Goalkeepers striving to excel at the elite level are obviously in love with the game of soccer. Chances are they're fans of the game and watch it on TV, in stadiums, and at their local parks. They might come early to their own games to watch some of the previous game, or they may stay after their game to watch the following match.

That's what coaches like to see in their players, because while the players are watching they're learning. And much can be learned outside of one's own games and training sessions. In addition to observation, keepers should be open to feedback and should be encouraged to self-analyze. These are all things that the coach can help with.

Watch the Game

Besides playing, one of the best ways for goalkeepers to learn to read the game is to watch other keepers. Keepers should attend as many soccer games of various levels as possible. They can learn from the great play and the mistakes of others. In particular, goalkeepers should seek out live high-quality play whenever possible. The keeper coach might even arrange to attend local events with the keepers and to discuss the action with them as it unfolds. However, the opportunity to watch high-quality keepers in live action may be limited in many areas, transportation may be difficult, or there may be other obstacles such as scheduling conflicts.

Fortunately, there's no shortage of soccer on television, and this makes it easy to watch top-level teams and their goalkeepers. But not all young soccer players are naturally drawn to watching soccer games, so coaches may have to encourage them.

To encourage players to watch soccer on television, coaches can casually discuss upcoming games and perhaps send e-mail reminders about when the games are being broadcast and on what channel. Try to get the team enthused about the games: "The United States is playing Mexico this Saturday in Azteca Stadium! Let me know what you thought of the game next Tuesday at practice. I want to know which team you think had the better goalkeeper!"

Better yet, coaches can watch games together with their players and debate angle play and positioning play. The coaches can point out systems of play used by successful teams or discuss the flaws that led to goals. Organizing team outings to watch games on television is good for team building. These outings also give players the chance to watch potential role models.

Modern computer technology enables coaches to e-mail clips of soccer games directly to their players. Highlights of saves are inspiring and instructional; a coach can include a comment such as the following: "See how the keeper cut down the angle on a breakaway and refused to be baited by a fake?" Clips can also serve as examples of what not to do. Coaches can send a YouTube link to footage of a goal conceded and can prompt a discussion on how the goalkeeper erred, if that was the case: "Was the positioning faulty? Did the keeper fail to direct his players properly on a corner kick?"

Coaches can even start a friendly pool or fantasy league to encourage their players to watch high-level soccer. Have players pick their favorite MLS teams—or teams from any league that is televised—and spur discussion on last weekend's games at the next team get-together.

Getting Feedback

Provided their egos can handle peer criticism, goalkeepers can get valuable input from their teammates, as well as their coaches, to improve their reading of the game. The keepers should ask the attacking players on their team about their goalkeeping. Here are some questions that a keeper may ask these players:

- What do you notice about my goalkeeping, positive or negative?
- What am I giving up?
- What am I not giving up?
- How difficult am I to beat?
- Where do you aim to give yourself the best chance of scoring on me?

Keepers should also talk with their coaches about the sport and players as much as possible. Watching game footage together and analyzing play are an excellent way to develop a feel for the game and to comprehend the various ways that attackers try to beat goalkeepers.

Writing It Down

Goalkeepers should have a notebook in which they log information about their play in games and their practice routines. A good old-fashioned paper notebook works just fine, but this can be done on the computer as well.

VIDEO TESTING

Show your goalkeepers some video of the buildup to an attack during a game they haven't seen yet. Pause the action right before the attacker is faced with a critical decision. For example, a player dribbles past a wide midfielder, has one defender to beat, and has the option to shoot, cross, or take on another defender.

With the action paused, ask the keepers to identify three choices the attacker has and to list these choices as (1) most logical, (2) somewhat likely, and (3) least likely. This exercise helps keepers recognize how plays can unfold. Of course, soccer is an unpredictable game, and the most brilliant players are capable of pulling off surprise moves with success. But by watching the game like this, keepers exercise their minds to prepare for all the options. Doing so in off-field exercises helps them bring confidence to the field.

After a game, the keepers should write down all the saves they made and all the goals they gave up so they can go back and recognize trends. A goalkeeper may read through his notebook and realize that he's been giving up breakaways in game after game. This indicates not only that he needs to practice stopping breakaways, but also that he needs to reevaluate his starting position and work with his back line on preventing breakaways.

The notebook enables the goalkeeper to track his play individually and analyze where work needs to be done while also helping within the team. Why is the team giving up chances? Identifying what kind of chances the team is giving up makes it easier to address the problems.

TARGETED TRAINING

Having identified patterns and problematic situations, keepers (and their teammates) can focus on those areas in training. The following sections address two common areas of difficulty: breakaways and defensive battles directly in front of the goal.

Breakaways

Sudden breakaways can be challenging. Keepers who formulate and practice a strategy and who use proper technique will be prepared to thwart a one-on-one attack on game day. A good starting spot comes from carefully monitoring play and understanding how to play the angles (see chapter 4). From a sprinter's position, the keeper should take several explosive steps toward the ball, then lower her body. The keeper should strive to present a long barrier along the ground to take up as much space as possible. The chest should meet the ball, the legs should be behind the body, and the hands should wrap around the ball. The keeper should keep her head down to avoid getting clipped by the opponent as she jumps over or runs past the keeper.

The breakaway exercises that follow need to be performed in a soft grassy area. It doesn't need to be the goal area, although that is the optimal location. Limit the number of repetitions for *all* breakaway situations to a maximum of six to eight. Proper technique is important to ensure that the keeper doesn't get injured. With too many repetitions, the technique tends to break down, and the risk of injury goes up.

Breakaway Preparation

In this exercise, the keeper works on exploding to the ball, getting low, creating a long barrier, and bringing the chest to the ball.

Setup

Place a ball 10 yards from the keeper. Use cones to mark the keeper's starting position.

Procedure

The keeper starts in a sprinter's stance and moves explosively toward the ball, which is stationary *(a)*. As the keeper approaches the ball, he lowers his body and slides

on his side, presenting a long barrier at the ball *(b)*. The keeper hits the ball with *only* his chest and uses the momentum of the approach to push the ball away *(c)*. Then the keeper returns to the starting spot to begin again.

Repetitions

After three or four strikes on the ball, the keeper should practice sliding onto the other side for the same number of strikes on the ball.

Variations

The keeper performs the same exercise but now catches the ball in the hands.

Breakaway Trio

These exercises present three different scenarios in which goalkeepers can save a breakaway: snatching the ball when it gets away from the attacker; taking the ball off the opponent's foot before a shot; and making the save after the attacker has shot the ball. All three exercises are designed to give keepers confidence in 1v1 situations. The exercises should be performed to both sides.

Exercise 1: Snatching the Loose Ball

The attacker should go at 50 percent speed until directed otherwise by the coach.

Setup

The goalkeeper starts 10 yards from server 1, who has the ball at his feet. Use cones to mark the keeper's starting position.

Procedure

Server 1 takes a soft touch. The second touch is heavy, and the ball rolls between the server and the keeper *(a)*. This signals that the keeper can come off the line to snatch the ball. The keeper collects the ball using a breakaway technique *(b)*.

(continued)

Exercise 1: Snatching the Loose Ball *(continued)*

Repetitions

Perform four to six snatches on each side.

Exercise 2: Stealing the Ball off the Attacker's Feet

Setup

The goalkeeper starts 10 yards from server 1, who has the ball at his feet. Use cones to mark the keeper's starting position.

Procedure

Server 1 begins the exercise by dribbling at the keeper *(a)*. When server 1 lowers his head to look at the ball, this keys the keeper to come off his line. The goalkeeper slides through the ball and takes the ball off the attacker's foot *(b)*.

Repetitions

Perform four to six steals to each side.

Exercise 3: Saving the Shot

Setup

The goalkeeper starts 10 yards from server 1, who has the ball at his feet. Use cones to mark the keeper's starting position.

Procedure

Server 1 dribbles at the keeper. The keeper closes down server 1 *(a)* and begins to slide at server 1's feet. As the keeper is sliding at server 1's feet, server 1 shoots the ball directly into the keeper *(b)*.

Repetitions

Perform four to six saves to each side.

Breakaway Simulation in the Goal

Vary the starting positions of the servers so that server 1 attacks the keeper's right, left, and center. Servers should start from various distances to simulate game-like conditions.

Setup

The goalkeeper begins in the goal with the ball at his feet. Server 1 is 20 to 25 yards away and roughly aligned with the keeper. Server 2 is a few yards closer to the goal but off to one side.

Procedure

Using his feet, the goalkeeper serves the ball to server 1. Server 1 plays the ball between server 2 and the keeper or to the feet of server 2. Server 2 receives the ball and attacks the keeper at match pace on a breakaway. The keeper decides how to defend and makes his move—snatching the loose ball, taking the ball off the attacker's feet, or saving the shot. After the keeper makes the play, the exercise begins again.

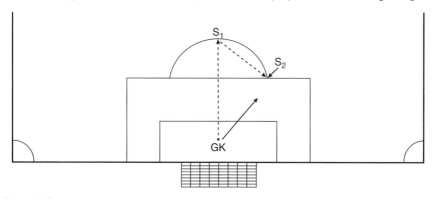

Repetitions

Perform six to eight repetitions maximum.

Breakaway Checklist

Here are some tactical decisions that the keeper must consider when coping with a breakaway:

- Has the attacker lost control of the ball?
- What is the speed of the attacker coming at the goal?
- Where is the attacker on the field?
- Where are the defenders?
- What are the strengths and tendencies of the attacker? Is this player more likely to dribble and try to get around the keeper or to shoot it?
- Can the keeper close distance as the attacker puts his head down?
- What angle of the goal is the attacker coming from?
- What is the best starting spot for defending this attack?

Battles at the Goal

Goalmouth battles are a tricky challenge for keepers because they must cope with a crowd while they judge where and when to move. While concentrating on getting the ball, the keeper must be aware of the positioning and movements of teammates and opponents. Training should simulate actual battles at the goal.

Goalmouth Battles

In this intense exercise (and its variations), the goalkeepers work on their starting spot, communicating, supporting defenders, reading the game, stopping shots, and making decisions (i.e., when to come off the line).

Setup

Defenders start in two lines outside the goalposts. Attackers start in two lines outside the penalty area. The goalkeeper sets up in the goal.

Procedure

Defenders and attackers go 1v1 *(a)*. The defender (X) from the left side of the goal plays the ball to the attacker (O) from the right side of the goal; the defender then comes out to defend as the attacker goes for the goal. The keeper prepares for the shot—while doing so, the keeper should communicate with the defender about when to tackle. The keeper will usually want the tackle attempt to force the attacker away from the middle. Repeat the exercise, using a defender from the right side and an attacker from the left.

Repetitions

Continue alternating players from both sides of the goal for a total of six to eight battles.

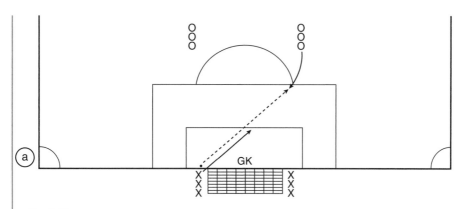

Variations

From the same setup, make it a 2v1. The defender plays the ball out to an attacker, who attacks with a teammate. The keeper must help the defender turn the situation into a 1v1. The keeper must anticipate and react to a shot, or she must read a pass and intercept. The keeper must act as a covering defender. The keeper always demands pressure on the ball from the defender.

From the same setup, make it a 2v2 *(b)*. Two defenders come out to meet two attackers. The keeper organizes the defenders, who must not get split. The keeper positions herself to provide balance for the defenders. The keeper should try to isolate the attacker with the ball.

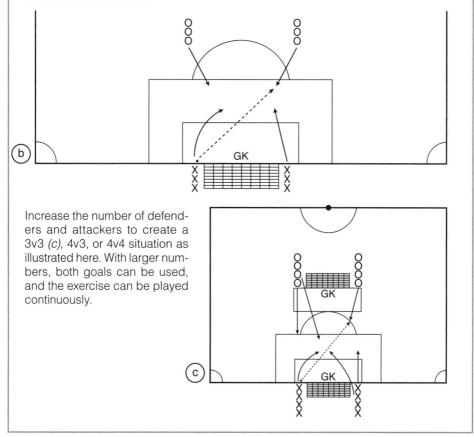

Increase the number of defenders and attackers to create a 3v3 *(c)*, 4v3, or 4v4 situation as illustrated here. With larger numbers, both goals can be used, and the exercise can be played continuously.

BETTER WITH AGE

What makes the goalkeeping position particularly challenging is that a team only needs one keeper, shrinking the opportunities to get on the field. But on the positive side, goalkeepers can have longer careers than field players if they compensate for the athleticism they lose with age by being an expert at reading the game. Here are some of the great elder statesmen of goalkeeping:

- **Dino Zoff.** The oldest keeper to win a World Cup—lifting the 1982 crown with Italy at age 40—Zoff played one more season with Juventus after winning the world title.

- **Kasey Keller.** Keller was the first American keeper to star in Europe, playing in the top-tier leagues of England, Spain, and Germany. He was still going strong in Major League Soccer as his 40th birthday approached.

- **Brad Friedel.** A U.S. World Cup veteran, Friedel had played nearly 300 English Premier League games for Blackburn when he moved to Aston Villa at age 37. Three years later, Friedel was still considered one of the EPL's top keepers.

- **Pat Jennings.** Jennings, who was Northern Ireland's keeper for more than two decades, played more than 750 English league games for Watford, Tottenham, and Arsenal. He played in the 1986 World Cup at age 41.

- **Edwin van der Sar.** The Dutchman represented his country 130 times, including games at the 2008 European Championship, where he served as team captain at age 37. He was starring in Manchester United's goal at age 40.

- **Hugo Gatti.** Nicknamed "El Loco," Gatti was a renowned penalty-kick stopper who played 26 seasons in the Argentine first division (from 1962 to 1988) before retiring at age 44. He won two Libertadores Cup titles with Boca Juniors while in his mid-30s.

- **Lev Yashin.** The "Black Spider" played in the 1966 World Cup a few months before his 37th birthday, helping the Soviet Union reach the semifinals, its best finish ever.

- **Peter Shilton.** The Englishman played 125 times for his national team. He holds the record for being the oldest World Cup captain—40 years and 292 days—set at the 1990 finals in Italy, where England finished fourth.

Catch Them if You Can: Handling Crosses

The ability to catch crosses is an absolute must for goalkeepers in the modern game. Goalkeepers who stick to the goal line put their teams at a major disadvantage. Attacking players are more athletic and bigger than ever, and they will finish many more chances to score if they don't have to cope with the goalkeeper going after high balls.

When a defender battles an attacker for a high ball, it is very much a 50-50 battle. And a well-hit cross improves the odds in the attacker's favor. But the goalkeeper, with the luxury of going after the ball with his hands, has a big advantage over the attacker.

Of course, attackers would rather battle a defender for a header than battle a goalkeeper. They know that the keeper has the advantage in such a matchup and may very well win the ball. A goalkeeper's ability to catch crosses may even force the opposing team to alter its attacking style. If the keeper is strong in the air, teams will have to serve balls farther away from the goal or try to create goal-scoring chances in another manner.

When goalkeepers establish themselves in the air, the defenders are spared the difficult task of battling for high balls deep in their penalty area. Knowing that the keeper can play off the line and claim crosses takes enormous pressure off the defenders and creates a tactical advantage for the keeper's team. By claiming balls that fly into the penalty area, the goalkeeper allows the team to defend higher upfield from the goal. This allows for earlier pressure on the ball and is much more difficult for the opponent to play against.

The keeper who snags a cross eliminates the scoring chance before the shot on goal, which is always preferable to having to save a close-range effort on the goal line. Catching a cross also makes it easier for the keeper to initiate a counterattack by throwing or kicking the ball to a teammate.

ESTABLISHING RANGE

Goalkeepers who intend to catch crosses must know their range. Keepers and their teammates must have a good sense of how far off the goal line the keepers can catch crosses. This enables the keeper and the defenders to coordinate their play. The greater the keeper's range, the higher up the defenders can play away from the goal. When the defenders play higher up, this allows the team to apply more pressure to the ball and makes the defense more difficult to play against.

Range will be established through trial and error. Young keepers should be encouraged to come out for any ball that they think they can reach. Even at the younger levels, keepers should rule the goal area. They will soon realize what balls they are capable of getting to and what balls should be left for defenders. Keepers should push their limits in practice from time to time as they progress in order to see how far they are capable of coming out to successfully intercept crosses.

Physical and psychological factors will help determine the range of the keeper. Height, strength, athleticism, and speed are advantageous. A tall, strong, athletic keeper with a good vertical jump and quick footwork should have the ability to catch crosses 6 to 12 yards off the line and in traffic.

The mind-set of the keeper is also very important in establishing range. To achieve their full range, keepers must be aggressive and must not worry about failure. Keepers who are worried about making mistakes coming off the line will play too cautiously and will force their team to defend deep into its penalty box.

The keeper must also be mentally prepared for contact and physical confrontations when coming out for crosses. Determination, bravery, and confidence will help keepers win these duels. Each win will strengthen the keeper's mind-set and intimidate the opponent into serving balls farther away from the goal, reducing or eliminating direct scoring chances off crosses.

Coaches should remind their keepers that, because they can use their hands, they have an advantage over the attackers when fighting for the ball. Keepers should develop a territorial mind-set: *This is my area!*

DETERMINING THE STARTING SPOT

Where the goalkeepers stand before they make a play on the ball significantly influences the extent of their range and the effectiveness of their play. Especially on crosses, correct starting spots are crucial. If the keeper starts correctly, he will have less distance to travel to claim crosses. This potential benefit encourages the keeper to come off the line.

Keepers are always hesitant when they have to travel a far distance from the goal. They think that the farther they venture, the more exposed the goal becomes. As a result, many keepers stay close to their goal line, and they're less likely to come out for crosses. And their reluctance to move farther out enables the opponent to serve dangerous balls deep into the penalty area.

A keeper who takes up the correct starting spot—several yards off his line whenever that's safe—will be more willing to come for crosses because he will be closer to the action and will need to travel only a *short* distance to claim the cross. A correct and aggressive starting spot will automatically increase the range of the keeper.

Remember that starting spots change every time the ball is played to another player. Goalkeepers must constantly monitor the action and adjust their position as needed to maintain readiness.

The first factor that determines the starting spot of the keeper is where the ball is located on the field. If the ball is farther up the field, the keeper can start higher off the line, assuming that there is no danger of the ball being chipped for a goal. Generally speaking, the closer the ball is to the end line, the nearer to the goal the keeper will start.

When the ball is at the halfway line or farther out, the keeper is positioned at the edge of the penalty area (figure 8.1*a*). The keeper retreats as the attack nears. If the ball goes to the wing, and the keeper is safe from being beaten with a shot to the near post, the keeper can remain a few yards off the line (figure 8.1*b*). In general, the ability to cover a near-post shot determines how far from the goal line the keeper should move. If an opponent has the ball 40 yards away from the end line, the keeper may be as far as 6 yards off the goal line if the keeper is athletic enough to retreat in time to reach a long-range chip.

Once the opponent launches the cross, the keeper has a split second to decide whether to go for it or prepare for the save. If the ball is crossed in as an outswinger (curving away from the keeper), regardless of whether the service comes from a high or deep location, the keeper should take an aggressive starting position off the goal line. It is safe to do this because there is no immediate danger of the ball going directly into the goal.

For an in-swinging cross (curving toward the goal), the keeper should play more conservatively and closer to the goal line. With this type of trajectory, there is immediate danger of the ball being served directly into the goal.

Some physical considerations will go into establishing a keeper's starting spot. Keepers need to be strong, explosive players with the ability to outjump the opponent. A good vertical jump is therefore required for a keeper to successfully handle crosses.

Figure 8.1 A smart but aggressive starting position is determined by a keeper's mobility and effectiveness as well as the location of the ball.

The keeper will need quick footwork in order to travel the required distance to catch or punch the cross. The keeper will also need to be agile to navigate through the traffic in the penalty area to get the ball that is crossed.

TAKING THE RIGHT STANCE

After establishing the best starting point for handling a cross, the next step is ensuring that the keeper uses the appropriate body shape and stance. The keeper needs to be in an athletic stance in order to quickly get to the ball and win it. Similar to when saving a shot, the keeper should be on the balls of the feet, with the knees bent, the arms at the waist, and the hands in the neutral position. The upper body should be tall with the shoulders facing the ball.

Make sure the keeper does not face the center of the field. Facing the center is called "opening up," and it allows an opponent to bump into the chest of the keeper, knocking him off balance and disrupting the catch as he is fighting for the cross.

Proponents of the open stance see this as the best way to organize the central and back-post areas of the field. However, preparing the body to deal with the ball is more important, and the keeper can use peripheral vision to track developments elsewhere in the goal area. It's far easier to fend off a challenge with the shoulder than with the chest. Therefore, the open stance should be avoided.

Figure 8.2 An athletic, angled stance allows the keeper to monitor the action and quickly shift into closeout mode.

Goalkeepers want to be in a stance at a 45-degree angle from the goal line and toward the ball—which means the keeper is leading with the shoulder—with a slight turn of the head to see the middle and far post (see figure 8.2). This position makes it easy for the keeper to move in all directions efficiently, and it enables the keeper to "close out" an opponent who is going for the ball by blocking that player's path to the ball.

To close out an opposing player, the keeper turns his shoulders square to the ball and occupies an area in the air between the ball and the opponent. Claiming this space helps the keeper win all physical duels.

FOOTWORK: WHERE IT STARTS

Once the keeper decides to come off the line, she has to move into the path of the ball as quickly as possible. Keepers want to *intercept* the ball before it reaches the opponent. This is achieved through proper footwork.

If the ball is arriving in front of the keeper, she can sprint directly toward it and adjust her final steps to set up her leap. If the ball is floating toward the far post, the keeper shuffles or takes crossover steps to move toward the ball. Meeting a cross requires the same footwork that a keeper employs to cover her area in other scenarios—moving forward, backward, and side to side—with the additional challenge of being ready to jump when the time comes to spring for the ball.

The keeper needs to have the ability to move quickly and efficiently in all directions: near post, center, and far post. The keeper must use quick shuffle steps as well as a crossover step to cover the necessary distance to the ball.

Footwork and agility are what enable the keeper to negotiate her way through traffic in the penalty area and arrive at the ball first. Keepers want to take a direct route to the ball so they will be able to jump and catch it at the highest point.

JUMPING: THE LAUNCH

The keeper's next action will be jumping to catch the ball. The footwork used by the keeper needs to prepare him to take off with one foot. Jumping off one foot ensures maximum power and explosion. Also, by jumping off one foot, the keeper will be able to protect himself and the ball from the opponent by bending the knee of the leg closest to the opponent. The technique is exactly the same as when going for a layup in basketball.

Soon after the cross is launched, the keeper predicts where the ball will be when he can catch it at its highest reachable point. The keeper jumps off the foot nearest to the goal (see figure 8.3). If the ball is coming from his left, he will jump off the left foot, bringing the right leg up to protect himself from the inrushing attacking players. (A cross from his right means he'll launch off the right foot and protect with the left leg.) The movement that began with a sprint, shuffle, or crossover movement ends with the final jump step, and the keeper explodes up and catches the cross.

Figure 8.3 A forceful, explosive jump puts the keeper in position to make a controlled catch while protecting the ball.

Keepers do not want to jump from a standing position. They always want to bring a physical force into the jump. By predicting the flight of the ball, the keeper knows when to take the steps forward that will allow him to jump through and over pressure. If circumstances prevent a forceful movement toward the ball, the keeper should try to take at least one step to create a launch. When that isn't possible (e.g., when a ball is deflected straight up into the air above the keeper), the keeper will need to bend his knees and try to create as much spring as possible.

CATCHING: EYES WORK WITH HANDS

Optimally, the keeper will catch the cross. For the keeper to snag the ball, the keeper's concentration must be solely on the ball. The keeper must be prepared to withstand pressure and contact from opponents while focusing on the ball.

Crosses are caught using the same technique as a regular shot. First, the keeper tracks the ball with the eyes, then opens the palms to the ball. The hands travel to the ball together. The keeper spreads the fingers and wraps them behind the ball, covering as much surface area as possible (see figure 8.4). The keeper bends the elbows to help cushion the catch. Bending the elbows also creates another level of protection against the opponent.

A keeper wants to catch crosses at the *highest point* in their flight that the keeper can reach because that is the point that is most likely unreachable for the opponents, who of course don't have the luxury of using their hands. Once the ball's downward trajectory hits a level at which an opponent can reach the ball with his head, the keeper's advantage is compromised. Timing the ball to make the catch at the highest point is especially important for shorter keepers because they have less of an advantage over the field players. The catch is completed by looking the ball directly into the hands. Total concentration is required!

Figure 8.4 With practice, keepers can develop the concentration to time the catch properly and use good form while under pressure.

PUNCHING: THE NEXT BEST OPTION

Sometimes the goalkeeper will simply not be able to catch the cross. At such times, the keeper will opt to punch the ball to safety.

The preliminary punching technique is exactly the same as for catching the cross—that is, the same footwork and jumping method—but the keeper makes a fist to punch the ball away. Ideally, the keeper will punch the ball with two fists (see figure 8.5*a*), but at times the keeper might be forced to use only one fist because of the player traffic and the path of the ball (see figure 8.5*b*). When

Figure 8.5 When a cross cannot be caught, a powerful *(a)* two-fisted or *(b)* one-fisted punch can be used to clear the ball from the goal and give the defense a chance to reset.

a keeper is punching with one hand, the opposite arm should be bent and up off the body. This creates balance and protection.

The keeper should create a flat and large surface area to make contact with the ball. The elbows are bent, and the punch comes from the chest. Keepers should pull the hands in and up to the chest to prepare for the punch. This creates the power and distance needed to get the ball safely away.

The best way to maximize the impact of the punch is to send the ball back in the direction from which it came. But sometimes the flight of the ball requires the keeper to punch the ball in the direction it is flying. The main objective is to get the ball out of immediate danger.

The following exercises allow keepers to practice the footwork, jumping, and catching skills that go into defending the cross. Training in a goal with proper markings for the penalty box gives the keeper an idea of his range for claiming crosses.

Defending the Cross Warm-Up Exercises

Basic Warm-Up

Setup

Place two cones in the goal area 1 yard inside each post and 4 yards off the goal line. Two servers stand 5 yards in front of the cones, each with a supply of balls. The goalkeeper sets up in the goal.

Procedure

The goalkeeper saves a chest-high volley from server 1. The keeper then moves across and saves a high ball from server 2.

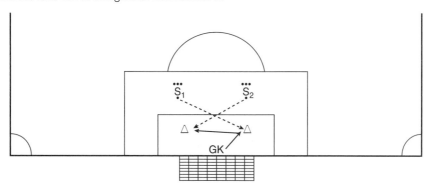

Repetitions

After each server has sent eight to ten balls to the keeper, the servers switch sides and send another eight to ten.

Variation

Have two keepers train simultaneously. Each keeper sets up across from each server, and the keepers exchange positions after each serve. This forces keepers to function under pressure and to focus even more on footwork.

(continued)

Defending the Cross Warm-Up Exercises *(continued)*

Extended Warm-Up

In this exercise, keepers work on their footwork and range as well as their ability to save high balls at the near post, centrally, and at the back post. The exercise trains the keepers' ability to read the flight of the ball and make adjustments.

Setup

Place three cones across the goal, one at the near post 4 yards off the goal line, one on the middle of the goal box line (6 yards out), and the third at the back post 4 yards off the goal line. One server begins at the end line just outside the goal area (6 yards from the post). A second server is positioned diagonally off the corner of the goal area, 10 yards off the goal line.

Procedure

The goalkeeper saves a chest-high volley from server 1 at the near post, then drops off the near post. Server 2 serves a high ball to the cone placed in front of the near post, and the goalkeeper attacks and catches it. The keeper then returns to the near post to save a volley from server 1. The keeper drops off the near post and uses crossover footwork to return to the middle and save a high ball from server 2. The keeper again returns to the near post to save a volley. The keeper then uses crossover steps to cover the distance to the back post and save a high ball from server 2.

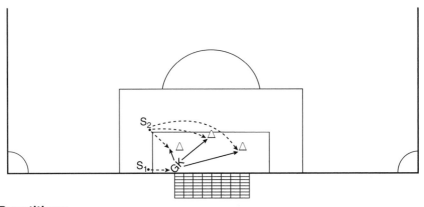

Repetitions

After three full sets, the keeper rests while another keeper trains. Then the servers move to the other side of the goal, and the sequence is repeated.

DECISION MAKING

Once the technical components of dealing with crosses have been mastered, the focus shifts to tactical considerations and the most difficult part of goalkeeping: decision making.

Given enough proper training, all keepers will be solid shot stoppers and will possess the necessary skill set to be functional in goal. But being a top-flight goalkeeper comes down to making *correct* decisions. This is why keepers generally reach their peak in their early 30s. By then they have acquired enough game and training experience to make correct decisions.

When a keeper is dealing with crosses, the key decisions include determining the proper starting position, reading the flight of the ball, and gauging whether the cross is reachable.

COUNTERINTELLIGENCE:
THE BECKHAM CROSS

Fortunately for goalkeepers, many players deliver crosses blindly. As British commentators are apt to say, these players "whip the ball into the mixer" and hope for the best. Smart players realize that a cross is still a pass and should be aimed to an area where an attacking teammate has a good chance of meeting it.

David Beckham is a good example of a crosser who looks for his teammates before he strikes the ball. From his right wing, Beckham's cross bends away from the goalkeeper and into the path of the attacker, which forces the keeper to chase the ball and gives the attacker the advantage. The attacker is running into the ball and can put the energy generated by that movement into the header.

will benson/Marka/age fotostock

Figure 8.6 David Beckham consistently delivers a purposeful cross, bending it toward an attacking teammate and away from the keeper.

The challenge for the goalkeeper is to keep one eye on the attacking players who are running toward the goal and the other eye on the crosser's approach. Knowing who and where the crosser's targets are enables the keeper to make the best decision on whether to leave his line for the ball or prepare for the shot (if the defenders don't clear the threat).

Getting Into Position

Where the keeper is positioned when a cross is served will be a crucial factor in the keeper's decision on whether to come out and claim the cross or to stay on the line and await the shot. If the keeper can establish a high starting spot before the cross, and if the keeper is close to where the ball is aimed, he will have a greater chance of making the correct decision. Being close to the play enables the keeper to better evaluate the service and make a smart decision.

Remember, the less distance the keeper has to travel from the goal to reach the ball, the more willing the keeper will be to go after a cross—and the greater the chance of reaching the ball in time to make a play. If it becomes obvious that a cross will be an outswinger that tails away from the goal (the passer's movements will reveal this as he prepares to unleash the cross), the keeper can be more aggressive in moving away from the goal. Predicting whether the cross will be an in-swinger or an outswinger is simple. A player on the right wing (to the keeper's left) crossing with his right foot will send in an outswinger. A left-footed cross from the right wing will be an in-swinger.

The keeper needs to decide quickly if the service is within his range. The ball is moving away from the keeper, so each split second of hesitation decreases the chances of the keeper reaching the ball before an attacker does.

On in-swinging crosses, the path of the ball may be directly at the goal, so the keeper must be a bit more conservative. The keeper does have slightly more time to make a decision because the ball will be coming toward him—meaning less distance to travel.

As always, the starting spots are constantly being adjusted because of the movement of the ball. Experienced keepers also change their starting positions once the field player puts his head down to serve the ball. The keeper can do this because the field player has lost sight of the keeper. If the keeper is a few yards off the line before the player puts his head down, the player may think he can beat the keeper to the near post with an in-swinger. But while the field player has his head down, the keeper can retreat to cover the area that the player thought was open.

Reading the Ball's Flight

When a ball is served in by the opponent, the keeper must decide immediately if the ball is served flat or with air.

A flat service is one hit on a line with pace. The ball arrives in the intended area of the goal very quickly. Good players—for example, David Beckham, Ryan Giggs, Cristiano Ronaldo, Lionel Messi—hit crosses just like this. On these crosses, the decision is usually made for the keeper. These balls are hit with such pace and accuracy that the option of coming off the line is eliminated immediately for the keeper. Most of these services are intended to attack the near post or the central area of the goalmouth. With these types of services, the decision is easy: The keeper must stay on the line and make a play after the ball is served.

A service hit high and with air under it gives the keeper time to travel off the line and catch the cross. The intended targets for these types of balls are usually at the middle to far-post area of the goal. These services are often poorly hit by the opponent. Regardless of whether the ball is an in-swinging service or an outswinger, the keeper's decision on coming off the line will be based on the flight path of the ball.

The following exercises help the keepers develop the ability to read the flight of the ball quickly. Adding some pressure from opponents trains the keeper to handle balls under pressure.

Reading the Ball Exercises

Flight Path

Goalkeepers should be encouraged to test their range by coming out for most balls. Obstacles such as football tackling dummies can be used to simulate field players.

Setup

Two servers stand midway up the penalty area (9 yards) and outside the box (one on each side). Position three field players or cones in front of the goal to make the exercise more gamelike.

Procedure

The goalkeeper assumes a proper starting position and body shape for a service. Server 1 serves in a volley. The keeper reads the service from server 1 and either comes and claims the cross or takes a good angle in the goal. The keeper returns the ball back to server 1. The keeper then takes a position to save a high ball from server 2. The keeper makes the decision to stay or come out for the cross.

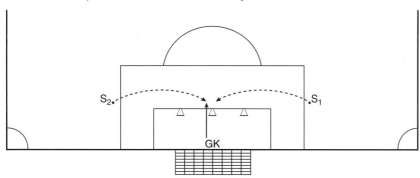

Repetitions

Perform three or four services per side.

Variations

Add a distribution component. Keepers send the ball to a midfield target after gaining possession.

Cross, Cross

A continuation of the previous drill (Flight Path), this exercise trains keepers to deal with crosses from wide areas. Servers should vary the service so that the keeper must field in-swingers and outswingers.

(continued)

Setup

Two servers (1 and 2) are wide at the corners, and two more (3 and 4) set up wide on the touchline across from the penalty area. Four field players (or dummies or cones) provide pressure in the box. The goalkeeper sets up in goal.

Procedure

The goalkeeper gets into position for a cross from server 1, who sends an in-swinger or outswinger toward the goal. The keeper catches the cross and distributes the ball to a wide player designated by the coach. The keeper then gets into position to catch a cross from server 2. The keeper catches the cross from server 2 and distributes the ball. Next, the keeper starts in a higher position to claim a cross from server 3 in a high and wide position. The keeper catches the cross and distributes the ball. Finally, the keeper gets into position and saves a cross from server 4 at a high and wide position.

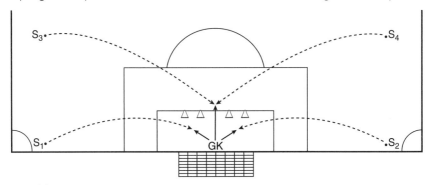

Repetitions

Perform eight to twelve crosses, alternating rounds of in-swingers and outswingers.

Cross, Cross, Shot

The keeper will deal with two crosses followed by a shot from the top of the penalty area.

Setup

Two servers are wide at the end lines. A shooter stands at the top of the penalty area.

Procedure

The goalkeeper catches a cross from server 1 and then distributes the ball to server 1 or server 2. The keeper catches a cross from server 2 and then distributes the ball to server 2 or server 1. The keeper saves a shot from server 3, and the sequence begins again.

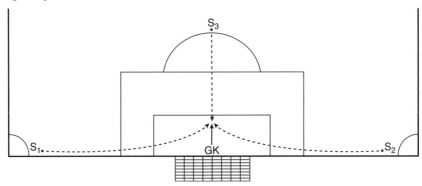

Repetitions

Continue until the keeper has handled eight shots from the penalty area.

Variation

Move the crossers off the end line.

Should I Stay or Should I Go?

Obviously, there will be players in the area when the cross is served. Why else would the ball be crossed? Before the ball is served, the keeper must have a clear picture of how many attacking players are in the box as well as how many defenders are in there to mark and defend the attacking players. The keeper at the highest tactical level will even know the qualities of the attacking players in the box at that time. When the play is developing, the keeper must know exactly who is in the penalty area. This will help the keeper organize the defense and identify the player for whom the cross is intended. Before the match, the team should have acquired thorough knowledge of the attacking qualities of its opponent. Who serves an effective cross and who is good in the air?

Don't be misled by size and assume that larger players have superior ability in the air. The 5-foot-7 Lionel Messi scored with a header in the 2009 Champions League final. Tim Cahill of Everton, though only 5-10, is excellent in the air. The "small" Brazilian attacking duo of Romario and Bebeto scored key goals with headers in their 1994 World Cup victory.

Having identified who is in the area, the keeper needs to read the runs and positioning of the opponent. This will also give the keeper a better understanding of where the ball will be served, and it will help the keeper establish the correct starting spot.

At the moment the ball is served, the keeper decides whether to hold the line or come and claim the ball. If the keeper chooses to come for the cross, she must use footwork and agility to navigate through the traffic to get to the cross. From there, the keeper's technique will make the play.

At times the penalty area will be too crowded for the keeper to come off the line. In some cases, too many players will be in the keeper's path to the ball. In other cases, a sufficient number of defenders may be present who can handle the situation without the keeper coming off the line.

When the keeper has decided not to come out for the cross, she shouts "Away!" This alerts the keeper's teammates that they are responsible for battling the cross and that they don't have to worry about getting in the keeper's way. The keeper follows the cross and predicts where it will be met if an attacker gets her head to it. The keeper moves to the part of the goal that gives her the most advantageous angle. She needs to be in the ready position when the ball reaches the attacker.

The keeper should let the game come to her. She does not need to go searching to make plays. All this will do is lead to unnecessary and potentially costly collisions. Keepers need to trust their teammates to make plays. A keeper should not come charging off the line in a cavalier fashion. This will only lead to goalkeeper errors.

Goalkeepers should come out for crosses only when they know they'll reach them. They must be confident but accurate in assessing their chance of success.

The following exercise trains the keeper to execute properly once the decision has been made not to come out for the cross; the keeper needs to drop back to the goal line and prepare to make a save or recover a second ball. The second exercise trains the keeper to make and execute decisions about how to handle crosses.

Stay or Go Exercises

Cross Recovery

The keeper must square his shoulders to the server and get into the proper body shape to make a play. He can use a crossover step to cover ground.

Setup

Place three cones about 5 yards apart to form a triangle: a "GK" cone that simulates the goal line and two forward (high) cones—cones 1 and 2. The goalkeeper begins near the GK cone. A server sets up across from the GK cone and about 8 yards away.

Procedure

The goalkeeper moves to cone 1, then retreats back to the middle cone to save a volley from the server. The keeper then moves to cone 2, retreats back to the middle, and saves another volley from the server. As the sequence is repeated, the server varies the service, sending low balls to the side (which require the keeper to collapse to make the save) and striking balls out of the hand (with pace) directly at the keeper.

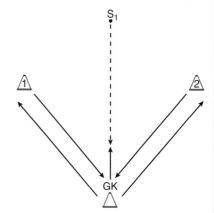

Repetitions

Perform eight to ten repetitions.

Two-Goal Crossing

This exercise gives keepers a chance to face crosses under live pressure and to practice starting spots, decision making, footwork, and catching or punching. Goalkeepers should use proper distribution techniques to return balls to the servers.

Setup

Place two goals 18 yards apart. Two servers are wide and deep, and two more are in high positions. A keeper sets up in each goal. Three players set up in the middle.

Procedure

The servers alternate sending balls toward each goal, and the middle players attack the service. Each time a ball is crossed, the goalkeeper makes the decision to catch, punch, or hold the line. Server 1 delivers a cross toward the first goal. Goalkeeper 1 handles the cross and returns the ball to server 1. Server 2 sends a cross to goalkeeper 2 in the opposite goal, who sends it back. Server 3, in a high position, sends a cross to goalkeeper 1, who returns it. Server 4 sends a cross to goalkeeper 2, who sends it back. The cycle repeats.

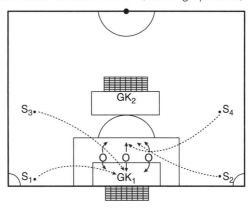

Repetitions

Do three bouts for a total of twelve crosses.

Variations

Change the goal that the servers play toward so that in-swingers and outswingers are launched from various positions. Add one or more defenders.

Ready? Set Play!

"When the ball is dead, the keeper really comes alive." That describes what should happen on set plays that threaten the goal. Set plays stop the flow of the game, if only briefly, and give the attacking team a chance to orchestrate a scoring opportunity. The goalkeeper must go to work to thwart the opponent's plans as soon as the referee makes the call.

Whether it's a free kick (and the wall needs to be set up) or a corner kick (and the defense needs to be positioned properly), the keeper must be calm, composed, and clear about what he wants his teammates to do in response to the call. The keeper's ability to quickly organize the team will play a major role in whether or not a goal is conceded. In today's game, players have the ability to curve a ball over the wall and to serve in a dangerous free kick that can be directed into the net off a foot or head.

Before the restart, the keeper must be sharp and alert—and must be ready to eliminate as much of the risk of a goal being scored as possible. How does a keeper limit the opponent's chances of scoring on set plays? He works on these plays during training and talks about them in team meetings. He rehearses where players need to be, the vocabulary that will be used, the roles that certain players will have, and the position that he will take up in the goal.

The keeper must assess the danger of free kicks that are within shooting distance and must set up a wall of teammates to protect the goal. He must provide the leadership that his defenders need to cope with free kicks and corner kicks that may be launched into the danger zone.

CONSTRUCTION BEGINS

As soon as the referee blows the whistle to acknowledge a foul, the keeper must immediately begin to analyze the situation. This is not a time to argue a call or to blame a teammate. It is simply a time to begin eliminating the chance of a goal being scored.

The first order of business is to judge whether the infraction is in an area that will allow for a strike on goal. Let's assume that it is within shooting distance of the goal and presents the opposition with a goal-scoring opportunity. The keeper must now organize the team accordingly.

The next job is to call for the number of players that will make up the wall. The keeper must be very clear, loud, and confident in announcing the desired number. This number will be based on several factors:

- Where the ball is located and at what distance from the goal
- The ability of the shooter
- The ability of the keeper

The more central the location of the free kick, the more defenders the keeper should place in the wall (see figure 9.1). In most cases, the total will not be less than two and will not exceed five. If the free kick is from fairly wide and the opponent brings only one player to the ball—and if the player is positioned for an outswinger—the defense may be able to defend the free kick with only one player. Players should practice and review the building of walls of assorted sizes so that the players know which players will assume which positions.

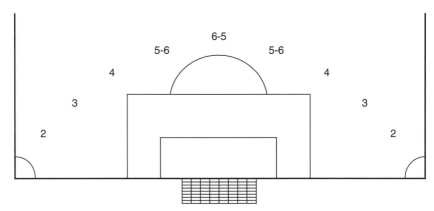

Figure 9.1 The arc of danger illustrates the relationship between the position of the ball and the number of players that should be used in the wall.

Once a keeper has called for a number, he needs to begin lining up the wall off the near post (see figure 9.2). When a foul is committed, a field player for the defensive team must stand in front of the ball to delay the free kick—without drawing a caution—in order to give the keeper a chance to get the wall together. The keeper stands at the near post and directs the placement of the first player.

Wall-Worthy Players The players who will be included in the wall—and the order of those players in the wall—should be determined at practice sessions and in pregame meetings. Going into the game, the keeper should know exactly which players will be used in all the possible free-kick situations that require a wall.

Figure 9.2   Assembling the five-man wall.

The first player in the wall needs to be someone who is usually on the field (a 90-minute player). In addition, this player should be someone who plays in a central location and can quickly take his place in the wall. Starting the wall with the same player ensures continuity between the keeper and the wall setup.

The wall will *always* be built off this first player, so the player must have a good understanding of what the keeper wants. That is why this player should be a constant in the number one position. He should turn his body to face the keeper so the keeper can guide him to the appropriate position. The keeper should set up this one player and then concentrate on the shooter.

The keeper needs to place the first player a full body width off the near post. Having this player overlap the post by the full width of his body rather than align between the near post and the ball will prevent the ball from being curved around the wall and into the near post. As players 2, 3, and 4 are added to the wall, the height of the wall should increase. Players 2 and 3 should be the tallest so that they will hinder a shooter from going over the top of the wall to the near post. Player 5 should also be tall enough to help prevent a ball from being curled into the upper corner off the far post. All these players need to have the courage to take a shot off their body to prevent a goal.

The wall needs to start about 8 to 10 yards away from the free kick. Any closer and the official will back the wall up, changing the angle of the wall.

Bullet Player   Because the wall is not an invincible barrier, the keeper's team should have an extra player or two at the ready (see figure 9.3). The bullet

Figure 9.3   Six from the middle.

player sets up off the last player in the wall (i.e., player 5)—he's not lined up in the wall but just off the last member of the wall. The bullet player's job is to block or disrupt the free kick. This player should move toward the ball at an angle that allows a window between the keeper and player 5. His approach to the shooter should eliminate a shot directly to the back post. The bullet player must have the speed to quickly close the distance to the shot, and he must have the courage to go straight at the ball as it is kicked. This player truly must take one for the team.

Weak-Side Cover   As the wall is being constructed, I prefer to have a player (usually a forward) stand behind the ball and adjust the wall for the keeper. This allows the keeper to set player 1 and then concentrate solely on the shooter. Once the wall is in place (see figure 9.3), this player covers the weak side or near-post side of the wall. Many opposing teams will run a player over the ball to the near post. If that area is not covered, the opponent will be able to play him in for a chance at goal. The weak-side cover player sets up off the shoulder of player 1. He protects that area and looks to clear a rebound after the shot.

GOALKEEPER'S ROLE

Once a foul is called, the keeper must spring in to action—not in a chaotic way, but in a professional manner. The keeper has to maintain and project an attitude that everything is OK and under control. The keeper calls out a number for the wall, sets up the first player, and takes up a position in the goal. Where is that position? This will depend on various factors, including how far away the ball is from the goal and whether it is left or right of center.

The keeper needs to be only about a yard off the goal line. She needs as much time as possible to read and react to the shot. This starting position will allow her to have that time. The keeper should be off the shoulder of the last player in the wall and should view the shot by looking between the last wall player and the bullet player.

Near Post–Far Post

The idea of setting up a wall is to try to eliminate the near-post option for the shooter as much as possible. The keeper is trying to force the shooter into a difficult shot. Many coaches believe that because the wall is designed to eliminate the near post, the keeper is only responsible for any shot hit to the back post. But keepers should try to save any shot they can!

Whether the ball is hit over the wall to the near post or hit toward the back post to the keeper's side of the wall, the keeper should make an attempt to save the shot. This is why the keeper plays off the last player in the wall; this position gives the keeper the best chance of saving a shot hit over the wall as well as one sent to the back post.

Shots that are hit over the wall toward the near post are difficult for the keeper for several reasons:

- These shots are usually curving away from the keeper.
- The keeper loses sight of the ball as it goes up and over the wall, making reaction difficult.
- These balls are often hit with fantastic precision.

Shots hit to the back post are usually hit with great pace, so the keeper faces the challenge of saving a ball hit with tremendous speed.

Importance of Scouting

Scouting the opponent is a very helpful tool for the goalkeeper. The use of video to observe the tendencies of upcoming opponents on free kicks is paramount to the keeper's preparation. How much scouting is done by attending games personally or by collecting video footage depends on the level of play. At the pro level, there's endless video available.

Video offers the advantage of allowing coaches and keepers to view numerous free kicks from the opponents so they can spot tendencies. They can also pause and rewind to check for helpful clues.

Scouting the opposition gives the keeper insight on where players are likely to put balls in specific situations. Should the keeper expect a right-footed or left-footed shot? Will a free kick likely be bent back over the wall or struck to the back post? Will the opposition use some form of deception to distract the keeper and the team?

All these questions can be answered by studying the opponent. The keeper needs to be fully familiar with a team's tendencies before facing them on the field in order to make the proper decisions and plays. A keeper should never be surprised by the way a team attacks a free kick.

When Opponents Meddle

Some opponents will add players to *your* wall. A five-person wall can end up being an eight-person wall if the other team tacks on three players to your wall. This presents a huge problem because it limits the keeper's ability to see the ball.

There is much debate regarding the best way to deal with players joining the wall. One idea is to put your players directly behind the attacking players in the wall. This is done in case the ball is purposely shot at the opponent's players in the wall, who then move in time for the ball to scream past them and into the net—in this scenario, the attacking players in the wall shield the keeper until the last split second. With defensive players behind the opponents, a ball sent toward an attacking player who breaks away from the wall would hit off the keeper's team and away from the goal.

Another strategy is to keep your wall small if you know that your opponent is going to add players. This prevents the possibility of winding up with an eight-person wall when the other team adds players. The reasoning here is that even though fewer players are in the wall, the keeper's ability to see the shot—which is the most important thing—is not compromised.

THE WALL: TO JUMP OR NOT TO JUMP

In 2008, I had the honor of being the goalkeeper coach for the U.S. Olympic team. Having defeated Japan, we faced the highly talented and favored Netherlands in our second game. After falling behind 1-0, we came back to take the lead 2-1 well into stoppage time. A foul was called against us, and a free kick from just outside the penalty area was awarded. This was the precise moment that our team's experience at the Olympic Games took a turn for the worse.

The foul occurred just outside the penalty area, to the right of our goalkeeper, Brad Guzan. This was a very dangerous position for a foul and presented a clear opportunity for the Netherlands. Brad did an excellent job of remaining calm and organizing a five-man wall, along with proper weak-side coverage as well as a bullet player. In a prematch meeting, we coaches had told our team that if the players who formed the wall were going to jump, they must not jump to a height at which a ball could go in underneath the wall.

The Dutch player Gerald Sibon lined up to take the free kick. He is a powerful and experienced striker. As Sibon ran up to the ball to shoot, our wall players jumped too high, and the ball went underneath the wall and into the goal. Brad had no chance to react to it. Instead of winning 2-1 and clinching second-round passage, we finished the game in a 2-2 draw, and we were eliminated after our third group game.

Brad Guzan in goal for the U.S. team at the 2008 Olympic Games.

Several aspects of this painful experience can be debated. Should players in a wall jump? Is there an advantage to jumping? The answers to these questions are not absolute.

In most cases, if the wall players are going to jump, they must make a unified effort not to allow the ball to slip underneath the wall. The most important thing is to wait until the ball is struck before jumping. The advantage to jumping is that the wall players may deflect a shot that is hit over the wall and is on its way into the goal.

One consideration that should never be overlooked when deciding whether to jump is the qualities of the player taking the free kick. If the player is skillful and hits the ball consistently over the wall, you may want to have the wall players jump. In the case of the Olympics, the player taking the kick was powerful and could be counted on to hit the ball with pace. When defending against this type of player, it may be beneficial for the wall players to stay on the ground, preventing a powerful shot from going through or under them.

DEFENDING WIDE SET PIECES

In today's game, service from the wide channels of the field has become an art. These are the balls that can curl into the box and, even if they are not touched, bounce into the goal. On set plays, balls launched from a wide field position are usually in-swingers. This kind of service can be very dangerous for the keeper. Teams serving in-swingers may bring their big players forward to create a very difficult defensive situation for the keeper.

In this situation, the keeper must take a position in the middle area of the goal in order to attempt to cover both the near and far post. The keeper should be no more than a yard or two off the line. This conservative approach gives the keeper more time to react to the service, especially if it is coming through a crowd. Some goalkeepers shift to the near post when they see opposing players making hard runs there. Keepers need to be disciplined and hold their position until the ball is served to avoid being duped by fakes and feints.

Depending on the location and distance of the wide free kick, the keeper should make sure that she has as much room as possible to come off the line—and to see the ball clearly. In most cases, this means that keepers will have their teammates begin defending from the 12- to 18-yard line. This gives the keeper plenty of room and time to make a play.

Some keepers who are very quick and strong in the air may push their defending line as high as the 18-yard line. The keeper should communicate the desired defending spots as soon as the foul is given. The defending team needs to hold the line and not allow the opponent to get in deep.

Once keepers decide where they want their defenders when defending a wide free kick, they must decide whether they want the defenders to use man-to-man or zone marking. The advantage of man-to-man is that everyone has a clear assignment. Using a two-player wall may force opponents to use a wider service.

When defending a free kick from the flank, most teams also keep a free player in the "hole." This player is usually in line with the near post. The positioning of this player counteracts the risk of a dangerous ball being whipped into the near post.

The five man markers begin from the 16 to 18 yard line to give the keeper room to come off the line. Defenders need to fight through screens and picks to stay with their players. See figure 9.4 for an example of man-to-man defense in this situation.

I prefer man-to-man marking in these situations because a zone defense requires sophisticated synchronization between defenders and creates too many opportunities for attackers to lose their markers. If the team chooses zone covering, then the players need to have proper spacing (two to three yards) across the back and must not allow players to run through.

When using a zone defense, the setup and coverage for the players on the ball and for the free player are the same as for man-to-man. The wall defenders $(X_4$ to $X_8)$ begin from a predetermined line and space themselves to prevent penetration; then they defend their assigned area.

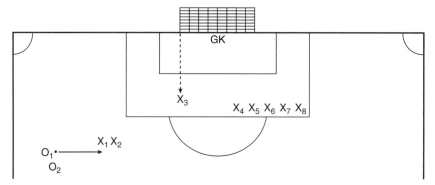

Figure 9.4 Defending against a wide free kick. If the second player on the ball at the kick (O_2) runs over the ball down the wing, the first defender on the ball at the kick (X_1) follows, and X_2 adjusts accordingly.

CORNER KICKS: HIGH ALERT

Corner kicks are a very good goal-scoring opportunity for your opponent. They give the opponent a free cross without pressure on the shooter. The keeper must be on high alert to quickly and calmly organize his team. Again, the keeper must not waste time disputing the call or arguing with a player. This is the time to concentrate and eliminate the danger of the corner kick. The keeper must ensure that the most vulnerable positions are defended.

Post Players An effective strategy is to have players on both posts during a corner kick. Too often, goals are conceded that would have been prevented if players were stationed at either post—players who could have cleared the ball to safety.

The post players will be most effective if they're standing with their weaker leg next to the post. In this position, the player's dominant leg is protecting more of the goal. For example, the player on the goalkeeper's right would be a left-footer—or at least a player with a strong left foot. This is a small detail that can make a big difference. Poor clearances after corner kicks often lead to goals. If the post player must clear the ball, the player should use the stronger foot.

The players whom the keeper orders to the posts will not be the biggest, best jumpers. Those players are needed to mark up and battle the attackers. The post players must be alert and have good, quick reactions.

The post players leave their stations only after the ball is cleared and the keeper has given them the instruction to "get out."

Free Players The next area that needs to be covered, or zoned, is the near post at the 6-yard line. Many teams attack this area. Putting a free player in this location (X_3 in figure 9.5a and 9.5b) helps eliminate this option for the attacking team. This player must be good in the air and must be smart enough to pick up players running in front of her.

Some teams also put a zonal or free player in the middle of the goal at the edge of the goal area (X_3 in figure 9.5a). This is done if the keeper's team is playing

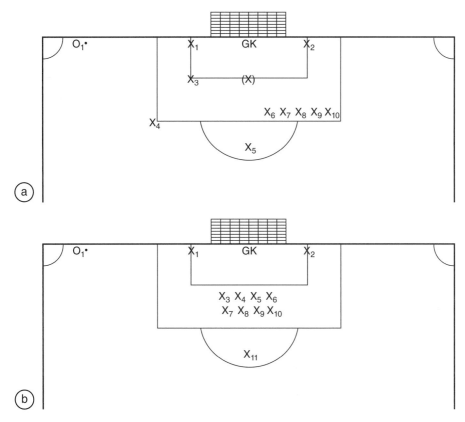

Figure 9.5 Defending the corner kick using *(a)* man-to-man coverage and *(b)* zone coverage. All players come back to the goal area to provide maximal coverage.

against a particularly dangerous set-play team, if the keeper has difficulty winning high balls in that area, or if the opposition sends only four players to the goal area. This player should be able to dominate in the air and should be very aggressive. Having a player in this position gives the keeper extra security, but it does make for a crowded penalty area.

Man Markers The next set of players—after the post players and the one or two free players—are the man markers. These players need to be combative and good in the air. They should be matched up with opposing players according to height, strength, and athletic ability. These players need to have a high level of concentration to stay with their player once the ball is served.

Full Cover The defending team must also cover the area at the top of the penalty area. Balls that get cleared out may fall in this area, and defenders must be there to pick up the scraps and not allow a strike on goal. Also, opponents may run a play where the ball is served to the top of the penalty area, and defenders in that area (X_4 and X_5 in figure 9.5a) can eliminate the danger. These defenders can also serve as an outlet for the keeper once he claims the ball and starts the attack.

COUNTERINTELLIGENCE: CORNER KICKS

Claudio Reyna, who represented the United States at four World Cups, took corner kicks for the national team and for the top-flight teams he played for in Germany, Scotland, and England. "Good corner kicks are very difficult for a goalkeeper to defend if they're delivered where they present the greatest danger, which I think is at the edge of the goal area," says Reyna in *More Than Goals* (Reyna with Woitalla, Champaign, IL; Human Kinetics, 2004). "A ball with a lot of pace that comes in six or seven yards from the goal puts the goalkeeper in a quandary. He must decide whether he should leave his goal unprotected and try to grab it amid the crowd of attackers and defenders, or to rely on his teammates and prepare for a close-range header or shot on goal."

Reyna says that the key to success for the attacking team on a corner kick is to have the three key zones—the near post, the middle, and the far post—manned by attackers when the ball arrives. "A perfect corner kick dips just before it reaches the header," Reyna says. "Without an arc on it, defenders have a better chance to get to it before it reaches an attacker."

Based on the way that the player taking the corner kick lines up, the goalkeeper will know whether the kick will be an in-swinger or an outswinger. Having noted which foot the kicker will use, in combination with where the kick is coming from, the keeper can prepare for the type of kick about to be launched.

"The advantage of the in-swinger is that the curve on the ball enables the player heading it to guide it toward the goal," Reyna says. "He's exploiting the momentum the ball already has. It's harder to head the outswinger, because the player has to get more power on it. And it's easier for the defender to attack the outswinging ball."

By watching the player's approach, the keeper can determine whether the corner kick will be an in-swinger or an outswinger—and thereby glean the first bit of information needed to decide whether to go after the ball or stay on the line.

Because very little time lapses between the corner-kick service and the arrival of the ball in front of the goal, the opponent's key attackers are usually marked man-on-man. Defending with a pure zone defense on a corner kick is likely to allow the attackers too much space as the defenders sort out who's marking whom. Teams that opt to use zone coverage must make sure the defenders are spaced close together and totally aware of when an opponent comes into their zone and must be covered.

Coping With a Keeper Menace

Some teams line up a player right next to the keeper on corner kicks to disrupt and distract the keeper and to strike in any ball that falls in front of the goal. This player needs to be defended. How the keeper's team deals with this player is very important.

Not surprisingly, the keeper often becomes preoccupied with the presence of the distracting player. Young keepers often get provoked into pushing and jostling for position. That's taking the bait. It's exactly what the opponent wants the keeper to do. Getting into a shoving match takes the keeper's focus away from the ball and the task of organizing the defenders.

In fact, this menacing player can be dealt with quite easily. The keeper should know in advance (thanks to scouting) that this player will be there. As a result, the keeper will be mentally prepared. The keeper should direct a teammate to mark this player man-to-man. The key to this tactic is the teammate's starting position. The defensive player needs to be on the *outside* of the opponent—not between him and the goal.

When the marking player is to the outside, this sandwiches the menacing player between the marker and the keeper, making it difficult for him to receive a direct ball. Also, having the marking player on the outside gives the keeper the room and space to come off the line.

Short-Corner Defending

Some teams elect to play corners short. Instead of serving the ball directly into the penalty area, the player taking the kick sends a short pass to a receiver just inside the corner, who then surveys the options for a pass. The defending team must be extremely organized and alert to eliminate this dangerous play. Keepers should have advanced knowledge of their opponent's tendencies in this area from their prematch scouting.

In general, if the opposition sends two players out to take the corner, then the defending team needs to send two players along with them. Which players go out to defend the short corner kick depends on each team's organization. Some teams have players leave the near post and top of the penalty area (players X_1 and X_4 in figure 9.6) to cover it. Regardless of which players are selected to diffuse the situation, the defense needs to have *even* numbers with the opponent.

Keepers need to be clear before the match on how they want short corner kicks defended. They also need to be able to adapt to a change if necessary. The positioning of the keeper will change with the moving and playing of the ball.

CONSTANT REHEARSAL

Set pieces decide games at all levels. Keepers need to constantly rehearse defending set plays on the training ground. Set plays also need to be discussed and analyzed in video sessions and meetings.

Scouting is an important component to defending and preventing goals on set pieces. Keepers must have thorough knowledge about where an opponent tends to attack on a corner kick and where a player is likely to shoot on a free kick. With this information, the keeper can organize the defenders with confidence.

Composure, communication, organization, fundamental skills, and experience in confronting set plays are the ingredients to preventing free kicks and corner kicks from turning into goals. Teams should design their strategy for defending set plays based on the comfort and characteristics of the keeper and the team.

chapter 10

In the Spotlight: Penalty Kicks

Saving a penalty kick is one of the goalkeeper's greatest feats. The shooter gets a crack from only 12 yards away, stacking the odds greatly against the keeper. Various studies indicate that about 80 percent of penalty kicks at all levels result in goals.

But when the keeper saves a penalty kick, it provides a huge motivational boost for his team while delivering a big dose of disappointment for the opponent. Then, of course, there are the penalty-kick tiebreakers used in knockout competitions. Two of the last five men's World Cup finals have been settled by penalty kicks, and the U.S. women lifted their historic 1999 World Cup crown at the Rose Bowl thanks to a penalty-kick shootout.

So great is the advantage that the shooter has when taking a penalty kick that goalkeepers usually have to guess to what side the shooter will aim at, then throw their body in that direction. If the goalkeeper waits until the kick is taken—and it's a well-hit, well-aimed strike—the keeper won't be able to reach it. Thus, the penalty kick launches the psychological battle so well described in Peter Handke's novel *The Goalie's Anxiety at the Penalty Kick* (London: Quartet Books, 1978).

> The goalkeeper is trying to work out which corner the man taking the kick will aim for. If he knows the player, he knows which corner he usually goes for. But probably the man taking the penalty is also reckoning that the goalie has worked this out himself. So the goalie has to go on working out that just today the ball might go into the other corner. But what if the man taking the kick follows the goalkeeper's thinking and plans to shoot in the usual corner after all? And so on, and so on.

Simply guessing correctly on the direction of the shot is only part of the keeper's challenge. The keeper still has to make the save. But even if the penalty kick significantly favors the shooter, good preparation and training will help even the odds for the keeper.

Silke Rottenberg exudes confidence and readiness in the face of pressure.

THE REF POINTS TO THE SPOT

Saving a penalty kick during a game and saving a penalty kick in a shootout are two entirely different things. The penalty kick in the game is a one-off situation. The keeper must use her power of observation and her knowledge of the opponent's history. She must assess the type of player taking the kick and consider the score and time of the match. And, finally, the keeper must have nerves of steel.

When a penalty kick is called during a game, if the team accused of incurring the penalty sprints to the referee to argue, the keeper needs to stay out of the fray! The keeper needs to use all available time after the call to focus on saving the penalty kick. She must remain calm and review the situation—and get ready.

BEWARE OF DECEPTION

On a penalty kick, some goalkeepers may think that they can get useful clues on how the shooter will aim by watching the shooter's eye or head movements. Tim Howard doesn't think so, and he warns that trying to do so may send the keeper into the shooter's trap.

"In the run of play, when a shooter bears down on you, the keeper may read signs from the player's approach that reveal how he will shoot," says Howard. "But the penalty-kick situation is much different. The penalty-kick taker's body language is very calculated, very precise, and designed to deceive. Where the shooter looks, how he runs up to the ball, it's all calculated to put the keeper off."

Howard thinks that the keeper is better off relying on the information he has from the shooter's past efforts—and reminding himself that the real pressure is on the shooter, because the shooter knows he's expected to score.

In the 2009 English FA Cup semifinal, Tim Howard was the hero, saving the first two penalty kicks—from Manchester United's Dimitar Berbatov and Rio Ferdinand—to send Everton to the final. Howard credited studying videotape of the Man U shooters' tendencies with enabling him to stop the shots. He knew that Berbatov generally shoots to his left but that he takes a slow approach, hoping to force the keeper to reveal which side he'll dive to.

"I tried to be patient, which is really hard in that position because the goal is gaping," Howard said when describing how he waited as long as possible before diving to his right and blocking the shot.

Anticipating the Shot

Based on pregame scouting, the keeper should have had a chance to study a detailed report on who takes the penalty kicks, where those players usually aim (direction), and how they hit the ball (favoring placement or power). The keeper should have also taken the opportunity to review the opponent's history of penalty kicks on video (if available). When the day of the match arrives and the shooter lines up, the game of cat and mouse begins.

The player taking the kick probably knows that the keeper has been given scouting reports. Should the shooter stick to his favorite penalty kick or should he change? If the keeper gets the player to think in this way, then the keeper is winning the early part of the battle. Confident shooters usually hit the penalty kick exactly the same way every time, daring the keeper to save it. If the shooter has a seed of doubt about how and where the kick should go, this could lead to a mis-hit penalty. Keepers should remind themselves that it's the shooters who are under the most pressure and that very few shooters will approach the spot without at least some doubt in their mind.

If the keeper does not have past knowledge of the shooter, then he must use his power of observation. Is the shooter a skillful attacker or a big, tough defender? The skillful player presents the most problems. This player can shoot using various methods. He can curl the ball away from the keeper by shooting across his body, or he can "open up" and push the ball in the same direction as his approach.

With a skillful player, the keeper must ask the following questions: What kind of match is the player having? Has his touch been sharp? Has he been fighting the ball all game? If he has been sharp, the skillful player will likely shoot across his body (sending a right-footed shot to the keeper's right). If he has not been sharp with his technique during the match, this shooter may play it safe by opening up and pushing the ball at goal (sending a right-footed shot to the keeper's left).

If the shooter is a powerful player or a tough defender, the goalkeeper may anticipate a shot hit with pace without much concern for placement. In this situation, the goalkeeper doesn't guess a side; instead, the keeper waits for the shot.

The score and time of the match are an important consideration. In a closely contested match—with the game in the balance—some shooters will lose their nerve. They will try to safely hit the penalty kick on target. In a tight contest, many players will open up and push the shot to the same side as their approach. They may also wait to see if the keeper will move early and then gently hit the ball down the middle or in the opposite direction. That is why I tell keepers to hold the middle and make the shooter pick a side during closely contested games.

COUNTERINTELLIGENCE: ERIC WYNALDA

Eric Wynalda, one of the leading scorers in U.S. national team history, converted plenty of penalty kicks for his country and for his clubs in Germany and Major League Soccer.

Players taking a penalty kick are often told to choose what side they're shooting at and not to change their mind, because changing their mind and altering their mechanics at the last second can lead to a mis-kick. Wynalda didn't buy into that. He was confident that he could either force the keeper to reveal where he was going to dive before the shot was taken or keep the goalie glued to the line until it was too late for him to reach a well-hit shot.

"I figured that goalkeepers try to read where the shot is going when the shooter looks at the ball before the kick," Wynalda said. "So I learned to shoot without looking at the ball. I didn't need to look down, because I knew exactly where it was. And I left my options open until the last second."

The successful goalkeeper, even when he has already determined which side he will dive to, can cope with the Wynalda strategy by not starting his dive too soon. Because the keeper is allowed to move laterally on the goal line before the shot—as long as he doesn't move forward—the keeper can try to fake the shooter out with his foot movement.

Reacting to the Shot

After evaluating what kind of player is taking the penalty kick, the keeper determines whether the shooter is going to open up, go across, or hit the ball with pace. Then the keeper decides in advance which side, if any, he will be diving toward.

The best strategy for the keeper is to place the toes on the line, rock the body side to side, and then fake to one side and dive to the other. A fake may cause the shooter to change his mind when approaching the ball, leading to a poorly hit penalty kick.

The keeper must be careful not to give up the middle of the goal. Keepers should not leave the center too early when diving to make a save.

The keeper must never try to hold the ball. When the keeper attempts to grasp the ball and fails, the rebound will likely place the ball right in the path of the shooter to blast into the net. The keeper should use a strong hand or fist to push the ball to safety (see figure 10.1). In fact, the keeper can use any part of the body to make the save—body, legs, or feet.

Figure 10.1 Keepers must train the technique of pushing, rather than catching, the ball so that they can use it in situations such as penalty kicks, where the risk of an errant rebound being converted to a goal is high.

PENALTY-KICK SHOOTOUTS

The penalty-kick shootout (tiebreaker)—officially called "kicks from the penalty mark"—was introduced in the 1970s. The first major tournament decided by a shootout was the 1976 European Championship final, in which Czechoslovakia prevailed over West Germany. In the shootout tiebreaker, teams alternate taking five penalty kicks (or as many as needed after the first five until a winner is determined). This method was introduced because tie games became more common as soccer evolved into a lower-scoring, defense-minded game. Previous solutions to breaking ties in knockout competitions included extending overtime until a goal was scored, using the drastic coin flip method, and replaying the game on another day.

In 1982, the World Cup introduced the penalty-kick tiebreaker for its semifinal games (all previous games in that tournament were played in a group format in which ties were acceptable), and West Germany's defeat of France marked the first World Cup game decided from the spot. If the final, which Italy won 3-1, had ended in a tie, the game would have been replayed a couple days later.

By the 1986 World Cup, FIFA accepted the shootout even for the final. The final at the Mexico-hosted tournament was settled in regulation time—with Argentina beating West Germany 3-2—but three of the quarterfinals were decided by shootouts.

The first men's World Cup final to be decided on a penalty-kick shootout was the 1994 Brazil victory over Italy. Twelve years later, the Italians beat France in a shootout in the 2006 final. Since Major League Soccer's inception in 1996, two finals have been decided by a shootout. In 2009, both the MLS Cup (Real Salt Lake over Los Angeles) and the NCAA Division I men's final (Virginia over Akron) were decided from the penalty spot.

In 2008, when Spain emerged as the world's top-ranked men's national team, it too relied on a shootout to win the European Championship, having beaten Italy in a tiebreaker in the quarterfinals. On the other hand, some national teams have been plagued by the penalty-kick shootout. England was eliminated from World Cups by shootouts in 1990, 1998, and 2006. The Netherlands, one of the world's top national teams, was eliminated from three European Championships and one World Cup from 1992 to 2000.

Detractors of the shootout method point out that it decides games in a manner that has nothing to do with how the game is actually played—that it is an artificial way to determine a champion, or a lottery that overshadows all the play before it. Be that as it may, the shootout also increases the influence of the goalkeepers, often launching them into hero status for a save or two that sends their team to a championship.

Without question, shootouts place enormous pressure on goalkeepers. Coaches and keepers must formulate a strategy that allows keepers to approach shootouts feeling confident and well prepared.

Brad Friedel in action during the 2002 Olympic Games.

MODERN TECHNOLOGY

Goalkeepers and coaches have long studied video to prepare for penalty kicks. Usually this would be done during the days preceding a match. But the advent of portable media players has enabled keepers to have a quick study right before the shootout—as was revealed during the 2009 English League Cup final.

Eric Steele, Manchester United's keeper coach, had created a montage of penalty kicks by Tottenham players and had loaded it into his iPod. During the brief break before the shootout against Tottenham, United keeper Ben Foster watched Jamie O'Hara take a penalty kick in an England U21 match a few months before. In that match, O'Hara shot to the keeper's left. And when Foster faced him in the shootout, O'Hara again shot to the keeper's left, and Foster made the save. Man U won the shootout 4-1.

"It's an amazing tool to have, it means you can brush up straightaway," said Foster of the iPod in the *The Times of London,* "Ben Foster's iPod-Watching Raises the Bar for Manchester United," March 2, 2009).

My strategy for penalty-kick shootouts has evolved over the years as I've reflected on the experiences of the players I've coached. As a youth coach with Tim Howard as my keeper, these shootouts were money in the bank. Because of Tim's great athletic ability, I could just stand back and watch as he saved three of five or four of five penalty kicks.

While I was a college assistant coach at Rutgers University, we won a first-round NCAA tournament game against Columbia on a penalty-kick tiebreaker. Bill Andracki, our All-American keeper, saved kicks 3 and 4 for the win. On the previous kicks, we noticed that he moved too early. When he made the adjustment to hold and react, he made the saves.

In that same NCAA tournament, we lost the final to UCLA, 4-3, on penalty kicks. The Bruins' keeper was Brad Friedel, who went on to become one of the world's greatest penalty-kick stoppers. Friedel saved two penalty kicks in the 2002 World Cup alone.

Rutgers' shootout with Friedel was a unique situation because UCLA won the semifinal against North Carolina State the day before on penalty kicks. We knew the Bruins' shooters and the direction that they shot in. Andracki saved the first penalty. After that, they changed their penalty kicks and were spot on. UCLA was crowned national champion.

As a result of this series of events, I realized that it was important to study the mind-set of the shooters in order to help keepers stop the shot.

Shootout Strategy

A key incident in the shaping of my philosophy and the creation of my shootout strategy occurred when I worked as an assistant coach with the MetroStars, coaching with Carlos Alberto Parreira. Parreira was the head coach for Brazil when it beat Italy on penalties to win the World Cup in 1994. When I asked Parreira how he selected his shooters, he told me that he chose players "who could live with missing."

WHAT SCIENCE REVEALS

We should beware when the scientists try to tell us something about how soccer works, because the game always comes down to a battle of skills, and whoever is better on game day will succeed. But for what it's worth, here's what some studies have come up with on penalty kicks:

- According to a 2009 study by Liverpool's John Moores University (http://news. bbc.co.uk/sport2/hi/football/skills/4188836.stm), the perfect penalty kick is one that starts with a five- or six-step run-up, is struck at 65 miles per hour or more, and is hit at an angle of 20 to 30 degrees, which ensures that the ball crosses within 20 inches (50 cm) of the post, making it impossible for the goalkeeper to save. (Easier said than done!)

- In 2006 to 2008, Castrol conducted a study as part of its 2008 European Championship sponsorship (www.fifa.com/worldfootball/news/newsid=1086121. html). This study uncovered that 95.4 percent of on-target penalties struck in the air find the back of the net, while only 71.3 percent of kicks hit along the ground beat the keeper. (This doesn't tell us whether shooters who aim high miss the goal more often!)

- In a 2006 study by the Institute for Human Movement Sciences at Vrije University in Amsterdam (www.telegraph.co.uk/news/uknews/1521605/Science-of-penalties-England-take-note....html), chief researcher John van der Kamp concluded the following: "If a player places the ball just inside the post, then it is almost impossible for the keeper to reach it in time. The keeper needs about one second to get his hands to the area near the post—a ball kicked at an average speed of about 50 mph takes about half a second to reach the goal." (Obviously, that means the shooter has an edge!)

- A 2009 study by the Norwegian School of Sport Sciences (http://online.wsj. com/article/SB10001424052748704500604574485511765954716.html) found that the slower the shooter approaches the ball, the better the chances that he'll beat the keeper. The study found that players who took 1.1 seconds or less were successful 58.8 percent of the time. Those who took between 2.3 and 2.9 seconds scored 78.1 percent of the time. Shooters who started their rush forward immediately after the whistle (0.2 seconds or less) missed or were stifled at a rate of 42.6 percent compared to 18.9 percent for those who waited for at least 1.1 second before beginning their approach. (Keepers must keep their focus even when the shooters take their time.)

With that in mind, I approached MetroStars player Roberto Donadoni and asked him about the penalty kick he missed for Italy during the 1990 World Cup. After a brief pause, Roberto reminded me that he didn't miss the kick—the keeper saved it. There I had it. Players feel better after failing to convert a penalty kick if the keeper saves it. Missing the goal completely is the horror.

Armed with this information, I established a philosophy about penalty kicks and developed the following strategical tips for goalkeepers taking part in a shootout:

- Early in the shootout, players will take more risks. If the shooters are skillful, they may attempt to go across the keeper. However, the keeper should *never* leave too early and give them the middle of the goal.

- As the pressure grows, players will become more conservative. They will hit balls close to the middle or slightly off to the side. This will decrease the keeper's need to guess to make the save.

- As the shootout continues and pressure increases, players will take the safe route by opening up and pushing the ball to the corner. Keepers can read this as the player approaches his kick.

- Keepers shouldn't worry about technique. They must save the shot with whatever they can.

- Keepers should act as if they expect to save every kick. The keeper's own shooters will gain confidence from seeing the keeper's fearless approach.

I was pleased to see this approach work in action during the 2009 qualifying tournament for the U20 World Cup. My keeper with the team was Brian Perk, and in the semifinal against Trinidad and Tobago, Brian saved kicks 4 and 5. Both were hit down the middle. We won the shootout, 4-3.

HAVE NO FEAR

The shooter has a big advantage over the goalkeeper on a penalty kick. But that also means there's more pressure on the shooter than the goalkeeper.

Nobody wants to be remembered for failing to score on a penalty kick. So the shooter is likely to be nervous. The goal starts looking smaller and smaller when the stakes are high. A goalkeeper who has trained and prepared well can actually look forward to the penalty kick.

If the shooter scores, he's done what's expected. If the keeper saves, the keeper has beaten the odds and is a hero. To build up their confidence, goalkeepers should remember the penalty kicks that they've saved in past games and in practice. They should consider how much the shooter fears the failure. They should tell themselves, "This one's mine!"

Practice, Practice, Practice

A boy walks down a London street and stops a man to ask, "How do I get to Wembley Stadium?" The man looks down and says, "Practice, practice, practice!" This twist on the old Carnegie Hall joke highlights the fact that great performers reach the top of their chosen fields, whether it's the big stage or a full stadium of cheering fans, because they have worked on their craft tirelessly.

The great thing about soccer is that it's so much fun that players sometimes don't even notice how hard they're working. Good players relish the challenge of improving, and good coaches keep training activities interesting and fun and as much like the actual game as possible. The goalkeepers' practice time is split into two periods: individual training with the keeper coach and gamelike exercises with the team.

The technical portion of the practice, which comes first, is where the goalkeepers and keeper coach work on the specific technical requirements for playing in goal. These technical sessions should include a warm-up that builds into the training topic of the day. They usually last 30 to 45 minutes before the keeper joins the team.

To develop the tactical aspect of goalkeeping, keepers need to be put in a training environment that fosters the decision making they will face in a game. Much of this comes from small-sided matches in training.

TECHNICAL TRAINING: REPLICATE THE GAME

It is absolutely imperative for goalkeepers to get specialized technical training. It's how they acquire the skills that are unique to the position, and it's how they stay in top form throughout the season. Keeper exercises should hone skills in a realistic manner. That is, the training needs to replicate the situations that keepers will face in the game.

Arsenal goalkeeper Emma Byrne makes an athletic diving save.

Keeper coaches should avoid the gymnastics-type exercises that force the keepers to make movements they wouldn't make in a game. In all my years of watching games, I have yet to see keepers perform a forward roll or a cartwheel before saving a shot. The more correct repetitions of a particular skill that the keeper performs, the better he will become at it. Practical repetition develops strong technique.

Pure and Simple

Advanced goalkeepers in particular require training sessions that make sense within the context of the game. More experienced and more focused keepers will not respond to a bells-and-whistles approach to training. Exercises that are popular at goalkeeper camps that force keepers to perform tasks that aren't required during the game won't get the best performance from keepers during a match. Training for agility and athleticism doesn't require doing gymnastics maneuvers before making a save. The more closely a keeper's training simulates what happens in a game, the more likely it is that the keeper will be able to draw on that training during competition.

Keepers need exercises that either maintain their form or help them regain it. Practical exercises that require keepers to perform the exact techniques that they will need to use in the game are the most beneficial in this regard. A coach who cannot or does not put together a session of this type will lose the confidence of the keepers. Keepers count on the coach to help them feel fully prepared for the match.

A Collaborative Effort

A wise goalkeeper coach *anticipates and listens* to the needs of the goalkeeper. Coaches should plan training sessions based on what they perceive to be the

DISCIPLINE ON AND OFF THE FIELD

When Welsh goalkeeper Neville Southall started his pro career with English club Bury, he played so well in training sessions that the coach had to keep him out of team practice for stretches so the strikers could rebuild their confidence. Southall, who knew the importance of giving his all day in and day out, ended up representing his country 92 times in a career that lasted nearly two decades and included English Premier League and FA Cup titles with Everton.

Tim Howard, who turned pro at age 18, quickly comprehended that success depends on approaching each practice with focus and intensity. "It has to be 100 percent every time," said Howard. "At the highest level, everyone's got incredible talent and the ability to perform. The small things set you apart—the hard work and the extra work. Players don't always grasp that concept right away. I was very fortunate to be in a pro environment at a very young age and realize that it was a job, that it was cutthroat, and that I had to give a full effort every time. Someone's always trying to take your position or you are trying to take someone else's."

Kasey Keller embarked on his long, successful pro career at age 22 when he joined England's Millwall and found a party culture among his colleagues. But he avoided the temptation. "When you're new to a team, you can feel pressured to join," he told Mike Woitalla in an interview for a November 2002 article in *Soccer America* magazine. "That wasn't a problem for me. Besides not being much of a drinker, I found it easier to avoid it because I would spend time with [girlfriend and future wife] Kristen. It helps tremendously to have a secure base. ... Being young, stupid, and in London is a recipe for disaster."

Top-level players need to be wise about how to spend their off-field time. Their bodies need to recover from the rigorous demands of the sport. Said Howard, "The way you train, the way you eat, the way you go about your business off the field all contribute to how successful you will be. You have to have discipline and the right balance. You need to do fun things to put your mind at ease and relax. Everyone needs to let their hair down once in a while, but in moderation. More often than not, it's about being straight line, focused, head down, eat right, sleep right, train hard."

areas the keeper needs to work on to be successful while recognizing that the keeper may have different views on what would be most helpful. It is important for coaches to build a good relationship with their keepers, especially their senior keepers, and to ask them what they think they need in order to be sharp for a match. Keepers, in turn, have a responsibility to do more than passively accept the training laid out by the coach.

The coach and keeper should have respectful, constructive discussions on how to work together to improve the keeper's play. The coach should appreciate the goalkeeper's views while also presenting a case on where he sees a need for focus. The coach must always be able to explain why certain exercises are important. The keeper should offer specific reasons for the training she advocates and be able to point out its potential benefits.

Even some younger keepers can provide their coaches with insight into what they believe training should look like. Sharing ideas about training helps develop trust between the coach and keeper and also gives the keeper a sense of ownership over his play. Ultimately, the player, not the coach, is the one in goal who has to perform up to a certain standard. Keepers need to feel confident that their training has prepared them for the match.

Technical Training

The following components should be addressed during technical training:

- **Stance:** Assume the proper body shape (athletic stance). The most common error is hand placement. Make sure the keeper's hands start in a neutral position, waist high, open to the field. By the time goalkeepers are at the U18 level, they should have mastered this.

- **Footwork:** Use quick, fluid movement through the goal. This should include the development of a crossover step. Footwork needs to be trained in all sessions. Footwork technique continues to be refined at the U18 level.

- **Handling and catching:** Control the ball cleanly at all heights. This is achieved *only* through proper repetition. Older keepers should be able to catch balls that younger keepers need to punch. U18 keepers must strive for clean catching of balls hit with pace at all heights *and* distances.

- **Angle play:** Set up at proper angles in relation to the distance of the ball from the goal. This should be trained in *all* exercises. U16 goalkeepers begin to take more aggressive starting spots. At the U18 level, keepers need to establish higher, more aggressive angles to challenge the shooter.

- **Low and mid-range balls:** This is the most common save. Proper body shape and a direct path to the ball should be exhibited. Keepers make the proper choice of either catching or parrying these balls to safety.

- **Breakaways:** Take explosive first steps. Bring the chest and hands to the ball. Create a long barrier. Correct starting spot in relation to the ball is paramount. At U18 level, emphasis continues to be on proper technique as well as the reading and anticipation of through-balls.

- **Crosses:** This should start with proper starting spots for in-swinging and out-swinging crosses. Emphasis is on body shape (square up to the ball) and footwork to the near post, central area, and back post. At the U18 level, goalkeepers need to have an extended range of 10 to 12 yards. They need to handle cleanly and correctly (catch or punch) crosses in traffic from different angles.

- **Kicking, back pass, and distribution:** Goalkeepers must have distance and accuracy on goal kicks. They must play and clear balls with both feet and develop a punt, drop kick, and side volley. Keepers must be proficient at throwing and *never* losing possession for their team when they distribute with throws or rolling the ball. By the U18 level, keepers need significant range on all kicks. They have to be able to initiate a counterattack with both kicking and throwing. They need to be able to play the ball off all surfaces of *both* feet.

TACTICAL TRAINING: WORKING WITH THE TEAM

The tactical portion of training begins after the 30 to 45 minutes of goalkeeper-specific training. This is when the keeper joins the team. It is very important for the goalkeeper coach to remain with the keepers during this time to help them with decision making.

Training with the team is vital to developing the keeper's ability to read the game and take appropriate action. The coach should talk with the keeper about his decisions and his relationship with the players around him. Most keepers who reach the higher levels are high-quality shot stoppers, but the big-time keepers are the ones who master the tactical component of the game.

Tactical training can also be functional training: 1v1, 2v2, all the way up to 6v4, 7v5, and 8v6 situations, where the keeper plays behind the defenders and develops the ability to make correct decisions and to organize the team. These exercises encourage understanding between the keeper and the field players. These opportunities cannot be duplicated in goalkeeper-specific training.

Small-sided matches that emphasize various team techniques and tactics will also benefit the keeper greatly. An exercise that involves crossing in match conditions, for example, helps keepers learn to deal with crosses in a realistic setting.

Box Bumper Game

This is an all-time favorite for all teams. It's excellent for training keepers to save shots while dealing with distractions in their line of vision. The keepers are forced to make plenty of reaction saves, handle crosses, organize, distribute, and play with their feet.

Setup

Regulation-size goals are moved in to create a field about 40 yards long. The small size of the field creates frequent scoring chances. The field is marked off to match the width of the penalty area (44 yards). Each team has a keeper and nine field players.

Procedure

It's a 5v5 game in the middle area between the penalty boxes; players here have unlimited touches.

The eight players outside the boundaries are allowed two touches (one to control, one to serve).

Outside players on the flanks should hit crosses. Outside players behind the endlines and to the side of goals create goalmouth combinations and rebound situations.

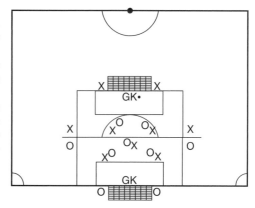

Rutgers Shooting Game

Several challenges are created by this exercise: saving shots from distance, dealing with rebounds, saving through a crowd, distribution, and playing with the feet.

Setup

Two goals are set up to face each other 36 to 40 yards apart. The playing area is the width of the penalty box (44 yards). Each team has a keeper and six field players.

Procedure

Two sets of field players are matched up 4v2 in the zone in front of each goalkeeper. For each team, four players stay back in their keeper's penalty box and cannot cross the halfway mark. They are to focus on long-distance shots. Their two teammates in the opposite box pressure their opponents to pass and shoot and look for rebounds, or passes they can convert into close-range shots.

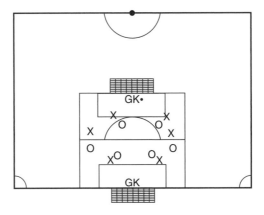

Small-sided games in which keepers are forced to make decisions will rapidly advance their ability. Whether or not they make the best decision, keepers learn from the experience. These games also keep the goalies active and force them to face the various challenges of a regulation game many times in a short period.

To develop the whole keeper, it is not enough just to bang balls at him and call it a day. Keepers need these small-sided matches to apply their technical work and to develop their tactical side. This is when a goalkeeper coach needs to be in tune with the keepers; the coach must analyze the plays that they make, pointing out flaws as well as successful moves in a motivational and instructive manner.

At the highest levels, team training is taped and the coach and player can review the decisions made by the keeper and make the necessary adjustments.

Tactical Training

The following components should be addressed during tactical training that simulates game play:

- **Stay or come decisions:** Make good decisions on when to come off the line and when to hold, which starts with taking proper starting spots. Learn to read and intercept through-balls.
- **Reading the game:** Master reading through-balls and reacting accordingly. Control two-thirds of the space behind the backs, which starts with taking proper starting spots. Make proper decisions on which crosses to claim and when to hold the line to make a save.
- **Organization of backs:** Use clear and concise language, including proper terminology: "away, push out, man on, mark up, pressure, and tackle." No cheerleading.
- **Organization of set pieces:** Direct the setup of a wall (numbers in wall) and organization of defending corners (ensure correct match-ups and zonal responsibilities).
- **Organization of team:** Take on a larger role as coach on the field. Give clear, composed, and concise directions to the entire team *when necessary.*
- **Anticipate the counterattack:** Recognize potential counterattack opportunities for the opponent while the team is still in possession, and organize players to prevent the threat.

WELL-ROUNDED TRAINING: TECHNICAL, TACTICAL, AND FUNCTIONAL

Exercises that test technique while putting keepers into realistic game conditions with teammates help them improve their game-reading acumen. Here are examples of training exercises that test a keeper's technical, tactical, and functional capabilities, all of which involve attacks on the goal. (The numbers for team size refer to field players. Attackers are listed first.) Table 11.1 on page 170 includes early season, midseason, and late season sample practice plans for high school age keepers.

- **Breakaway and save.** Exercises in which keepers work with a teammate against one or two attackers develop a keeper's technical ability to stop shots and thwart breakaways. Tactically, they make the keeper the second defender and demand clear communication. They also repeatedly require the goalkeeper to decide when to come off the line.

• **Defensive cohesion: 6v4, 7v5, 8v6.** Small-group exercises in which the keeper and four defenders, four defenders and a central midfielder, or four defenders and two central midfielders face a slightly larger set of attackers call for the keeper to read the game and manage the key defenders in high-pressure situations. It can include goalkeeper distribution.

• **Wing channel play.** This exercise, in which attacking players are sent down the wings, works on the field players' ability to cross balls, make runs in the box, and finish—all while testing the defenders and the keeper. The keeper must handle crosses and save shots, thus honing technical skills. Tactically, the keeper sharpens decision making, communication, and organizational skills.

Wing Channel Challenge

Setup

Field players compete 6v6 to 8v8, and each team places two additional wide players in the channel and a keeper in the goal. Goals are set up 60 yards apart. The full width of the field is used.

Procedure

The area outside the width of the penalty box is free; defenders cannot challenge the attackers in the wide channel. This promotes crosses. Inside the channel, players are restricted to one or two touches, forcing them to send the ball to the free area in the channels. Goals scored directly off crosses are worth 2 points.

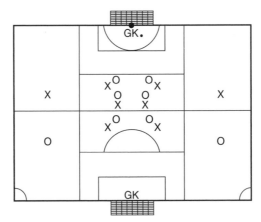

Variation

There's no touch number restriction on central players. Players are allowed to move freely into channels.

The numbers can vary from 3v3 to 8v8. In small-sided games the keeper uses not only his skill to prevent goals but also his knowledge of the game to eliminate scoring chances and to help his team create chances.

Bob Gansler Countergame

We used this with the MLS title-winning Kansas City team coached by Bob Gansler. This is a continuous game that trains keepers on organizing their defense against counterattacks, coordinating with teammates, saving shots, and launching counterattacks.

Setup

The whole team is used. The field size can vary (endline to midfield, or 80-yard field) but needs to allow for counterattacks by the attacking team and recovery by the defending team. Two goalkeepers are used. Flags are placed in a wide midfield position on each side of the field.

Procedure

The game starts with four attackers versus three defenders. One additional wide player for each team is stationed at the midfield flags. After the keeper makes a save or the defenders stop an attack, the ball is played to the wide player, who enters the play. The wide player and his teammates become attackers.

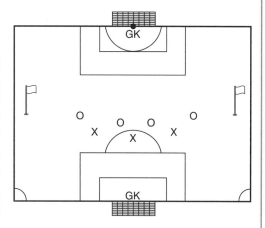

The four players who had been attacking are replaced by three teammates; these three are now defenders. The wide player must make the first pass back to his teammates and then the counterattack is on. The time it takes for the wide player to pass allows the defending players to get on the field.

Variation

The first attacker is allowed to go straight to goal.

General Training Guidelines (U16 and U18)

- The keeper needs 30 to 40 minutes of specialized training per session. This training should primarily consist of technical development.

- The exercises for the technical development of the keeper *must be match related*. They must simulate the actual techniques required in a match.

- The number of repetitions per exercise should be 8 to 10, *never* exceeding 10. Doing more than 10 repetitions turns the exercise into fitness training and causes a breakdown in technique.

- Use of video to show proper technique and decision making is recommended. Video can come from the keepers' own matches or from a high-level match.

- The tactical development should come from small-sided and 11v11 games with the team.

Table 11.1 Sample Practice Plans for High School Age Goalkeepers

Early season	
Warm-up:	
Stationary low balls Volley mid-range Rhythm work for low and mid-range balls	8-10 reps Stretching in between exercises Build to full intensity
Technical:	
Lateral footwork exercises with various service and technical demands: catching, saving low balls, saving mid-range balls, and saving balls off the ground right at keeper Shot-stopping exercises (Can also add in a crossing exercise at the end)	8-10 reps High intensity and concentration
Tactical:	
Small-sided games with teams: 5v5, 8v8, etc.	High-intensity games; 30 minutes
Functional:	30 minutes
6v4, 7v5, 8v6	
Midseason	
Warm-up:	
Forward footwork exercises for catching Stationary low balls Volley mid-range Forward footwork with multiple saves; volley then low ball; volley then mid-range	6-10 reps Stretching between bouts Build into intensity
Technical:	
Off the post series Milan low to high Milan high to low First-time saves	6-8 reps High intensity and concentration
Tactical:	
Small-sided matches Wing channel game Gansler countergame	Very high intensity and concentration Duration is up to the head coach
Functional:	
6v4, 7v5, 8v6, to countergoals	Duration is up to the head coach
Late Season	
Warm-up:	
Volleys, drop kicks, balls off the ground Stationary or over short set of cones Stationary low balls Rhythm work	Easy work 6 bouts max Stretching in between bouts
Technical:	
Basic shot stopping Crosses Kicking distribution	6 reps max High-quality but short work Maintenance work to keep goalkeeper sharp and in form

Late Season, *continued*	
Tactical:	
Bumper game	Emphasis on shot stopping
	Duration is 3-minute games or 2 goals
Functional:	
8v8 up to 11v11	Work with the players you would normally play with
	High concentration and intensity
	Approximately 20 minutes

chapter 12

Hitting the Peak:
Physical Conditioning

Being an elite goalkeeper requires being a 24/7 athlete. The decisions made every day at every hour have an effect on performance. Sleep, diet, and fluids in addition to proper training determine the degree of success. Among the most important choices a keeper makes are those that relate to physical conditioning.

Regardless of their current level of play or the level that keepers might be working toward, being in the best possible condition offers the best possible chance to excel. And those who wish to play at the highest level must keep in mind that the professional game is played by world-class athletes. Successful goalkeepers need extraordinary athleticism and discipline.

A goalkeeping coach can be of great value in putting together a physical conditioning regimen. Of course, the goalkeeper coach is a goalkeeper coach, not a conditioning coach. College and professional soccer teams have strength and conditioning coaches on staff, and keepers at those levels should take full advantage of their expertise. But even then, the keeper coach should work closely with the conditioning coaches to ensure that the training is suitable for the keeper.

The physical requirements for playing in the goal are much different than the requirements for playing field positions. Therefore, goalkeepers should be trained differently. Keepers and coaches who do not have a strength and conditioning coach can use the conditioning exercises and recommendations in this chapter to get, and keep, goalkeepers match fit.

In addressing the physical training, it's worthwhile to recall the physical requirements in keepers: anaerobic fitness, explosive power and vertical jumping ability, strength, speed and agility, eye–hand coordination, and quick reflexes. To play at the highest level and be competitive against field players, keepers must have most if not all of these attributes. Physical conditioning cannot increase a keeper's height, but it does develop and enhance the other essential qualities.

The first step in designing a conditioning program for keepers is to assess how the keepers rate at each of the physical components. This will determine how much physical training is needed and what should be emphasized. A conditioning program is essential no matter what shape the keepers are in. You need to evaluate fitness levels when athletes arrive for preseason to gauge how to construct a program that takes them to the required level in all areas by the start of the season. After the assessment, determine whether to train each component with the ball, without the ball, or both. And as the season progresses, constantly assess the keepers' progress and adjust conditioning training accordingly.

PRACTICAL ASSESSMENT

It's not necessary to perform specific conditioning tests, especially on young goalkeepers. How they perform in small-sided games and goalkeeper training exercises should indicate fitness levels and athletic strengths and weaknesses. As athletes work out with their peers, evaluate keepers in the following key areas and rank their aptitude on a simple scale (see table 12.1). Then prioritize their training, spending more time in the areas where they are least strong.

Table 12.1 Physical Conditioning Evaluation

Category	1	2	3	4	5
Anaerobic fitness					
Explosive power (jumping)					
Strength					
Speed and agility					
Eye–hand coordination and reflexes					

1 = very strong, 2 = strong, 3 = adequate, 4 = needs work, 5 = weak

• **Anaerobic fitness.** Goalkeepers don't need to go on long runs to play the position successfully. But they must be fit enough to handle the rigors of a full practice session or match without allowing fatigue to affect their play. You can tell whether keepers have the endurance to perform as field players during small-sided games or how well they hold up while performing multiple repetitions of goalkeeping exercises. Shot-stopping exercises are an excellent indicator of anaerobic fitness. If form starts to suffer shortly into an exercise, if footwork quickly gets sloppy, or if they get winded quickly, you know they haven't been training in the off-season. They will need conditioning exercises without the ball to build up fitness.

• **Explosive power and vertical jumping ability.** To gauge keepers' jumping ability, I like to watch them go up for crosses and high balls. Evaluate your keepers during drills, small-sided games, and scrimmages. If they misjudge the height or path of the ball, come up short, or are outjumped by field players, they need to work on their jumping skills. You can test keepers' vertical jump

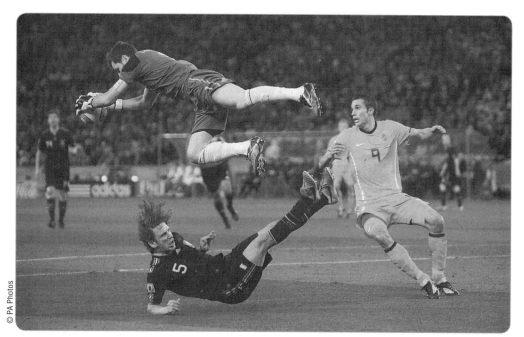

© PA Photos

Spain's Iker Casillas uses his explosive power and strength to claim a ball during 2010 World Cup play.

by measuring the distance between the top of the hand of the outstretched arm against the wall and how far up the wall the keeper can reach from a standing jump. I'm not inclined to assign specific numbers for a goalkeeper's ideal vertical jump. What matters most is that they can outjump field players. But vertical jump measurements are useful in gauging players' progress throughout the season. It can also inspire the goalkeepers to improve. A one-leg vertical jump that tests the keeper's strength with each leg is also recommended. The ultimate aim is explosive jumping ability off both sides.

• **Strength.** We want to develop goalkeepers, not bodybuilders. A goalkeeper needs to be strong in ways that suit the position, and this type of strength can be assessed by judging performance in challenges to win the ball. You can assess arm, leg, hand, and overall body strength by observing them in gamelike situations and crossing and shot-stopping exercises. Does the keeper not get up quickly enough after deflecting a shot? Is she shy to come out for crosses, perhaps for fear of being overpowered? Does he struggle to grasp the hard shot in his hands? A strength and conditioning coach can do specific strength analyses by monitoring weight-room work.

• **Speed and agility.** When the goalkeeper performs exercises in which he leaps over a series of small hurdles before making a save, you can sense if the speed and agility displayed match the requirements of the game. The keeper who has not stayed fit during the off-season will not be able to perform the series of movements to prepare for the save in a smooth and swift fashion. Pay special attention to how the keepers perform in the latter repetitions of an exercise.

• **Excellent eye–hand coordination and quick reflexes.** These qualities are less dependent on physical fitness. But a player who has spent too much time away from playing will not be as sharp. Watch the keeper's performance in practice for clues that further work in this area is needed.

ANAEROBIC FITNESS

Goalkeepers need to develop their anaerobic fitness level so that they can spring into action quickly and powerfully when the ball is sent their way. *Anaerobic* refers to strength, speed, and power, as opposed to aerobic (cardiorespiratory) fitness. Keepers need to have a healthy aerobic base because it helps prevent injury as intensive training begins. And although goalkeepers don't run all over the field, they must be immune from fatigue in order to remain sharp.

The focus of a goalkeeper's training needs to be on developing anaerobic fitness. The keeper should not be running long distances at a slow pace. She needs intense sprints that will develop fast-twitch muscle fibers, not the slow-twitch fibers developed by aerobic training. Anaerobic training is exercise in which the body operates with little oxygen replenishment. (Anaerobic literally means "without oxygen.") Anaerobic training is composed of short, intense bursts of work that replicate what keepers do in games. They perform movements at a high intensity over a short time.

Anaerobic fitness can be trained with and without the ball. The key is the intensity of the work, the duration of the work, and the rest intervals. The exercises should involve short, intense bouts with little recovery time. The work-to-rest ratio should be 1:1.

The optimal way to work on fitness is with exercises that also demand technique required in game play. The following exercise allows keepers to focus on fundamental goalkeeping skills while they are being challenged aerobically and anaerobically. Learning to maintain proper technique while battling fatigue increases the ability to consistently perform well—and it makes performing while not fatigued seem less challenging. Note that keepers do more repetitions during fitness training than when focusing on technique.

One advantage of anaerobic exercises with the ball is that goalkeepers enjoy them more. The ball brings fun to fitness work. It also means the keepers are training technique at the same time. And for youth team training, which doesn't involve daily practices, it's even more important for players to spend as much time with the ball as possible.

Keepers can do anaerobic training without the ball by running a series of sprints at a high intensity with little rest between sets. The distances of the sprints should vary, but they should relate to goalkeeping. Wind sprints, for example, can involve the keepers running from the goal line to the edge of the goal area and back, then to the penalty spot and back, and then to the edge of the penalty area and back.

Alternatively, keepers can run sprints in increments of 5 yards marked by cones (the longest no farther than 30 yards) to replicate the demands of the game. Remember to keep recovery times for wind sprints brief, maintaining a 1:1 work-to-rest ratio.

Turn, Save, Hustle

Not only are the goalkeepers getting physically fit, but they are also testing their agility and footwork while making saves.

Setup

Place two cones on the goal line, two yards in from either post. Server 1 begins at the edge of the goal area, set up to shoot a low ball in the area between the post and the cones closest to the post. Server 2 is at the 18-yard line facing the center of the goal.

Procedure

The goalkeeper starts at the post facing the corner flag. Server 1 serves a low ball, and the goalkeeper turns and saves it. The goalkeeper moves to the middle to save a shot from server 2. The goalkeeper then moves to the opposite post and faces the corner flag. Server 1, who has moved to the opposite side, sends a low shot to the area between the post and the cones closest to the post. The goalkeeper saves the shot from server 1.

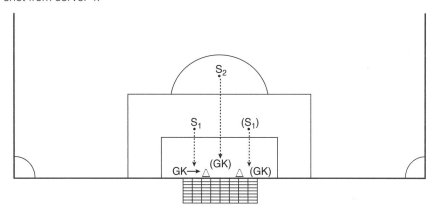

Repetitions

Perform 10 to 12 reps on each side.

Anaerobic fitness sessions should last 35 to 45 minutes. Any longer and you are exposing your athletes to injury. If you are training correctly, by the end of a 40- to 45-minute session, the keeper will be *done*!

EXPLOSIVE POWER AND VERTICAL JUMPING ABILITY

Plyometric training is a form of power training designed to produce fast, explosive movements by increasing the force and speed of muscle contractions. Plyometric training is excellent for goalkeepers because it can help them jump higher and quicker. Plyometric training can take many forms; as with other types of training, some exercises can be done without the ball and some with the ball.

Plyometric weight training should be done with the supervision of a strength and conditioning coach who can measure the stress to muscles and tendons and determine what an athlete is able to handle without the risk of injury. These exercises are performed in a weight room, usually by using Olympic lifts such as cleans, squats, squat jumps, and snatches. See the strength training section of this chapter for more information.

Jumping rope is a plyometric exercise that goalkeepers can do on their own in just about any indoor or outdoor location to improve their explosiveness and agility. Jumping rope works all of the leg and foot muscles while providing an anaerobic workout. And because keepers must stay in rhythm while jumping, this kind of exercise challenges them to maintain mental sharpness while battling fatigue. In fact, I have all my U.S. national team keepers warm up by jumping rope. Varying the types of jumps (one-foot, two-foot, and lateral jumps) and varying the intensity and duration keep things interesting.

Jump Rope Exercises

10-Minute Beginning Routine

Procedure

Begin with 2 minutes of continuous jumping at a comfortable pace. Perform 6 minutes of continuous jumping, alternating 30 seconds at fast pace, 30 seconds at slow pace. End by cooling down with 2 minutes of continuous jumping at a comfortable pace.

20-Minute Advanced Routine

Procedure

Begin by warming up with 5 minutes of continuous jumping at a comfortable pace. Perform 12 minutes of continuous jumping, alternating 1 minute at intense pace, 30 seconds at slow pace. Vary the type of jumping used in the 1-minute intervals: 1-foot jumps, lateral jumps, Ali shuffle (back-and-forth steps over rope). End by cooling down with 3 to 5 minutes of continuous jumping at a comfortable pace.

Plyometric training with the ball can involve jumping over minihurdles before performing an exercise. Use 6-inch-high minihurdles for young players and 12-inch hurdles for older, bigger players. If you do not have hurdles, use a rope. The rope should be set at a height that is challenging but allows for the use of proper form while jumping and while performing a keeper action. These heights will vary based on the age, size, and athletic ability of the keeper. Cones can also be used. I love to use these exercises in preseason. It brings the weight-room work onto the field.

Bounding over an obstacle and performing a goalkeeper skill combine physical training with technical training. I use short repetitions (four or five) because I want to create power. You can alter the sample exercise that follows by varying the placement of the servers and the type of shot delivered.

Jumping and Saving

Setup

Place three minihurdles or cones (use cones for younger players) across the front of the goal, within half of the goal frame but far enough apart to allow for landing and jumping. Server 1 begins 18 yards out at the edge of penalty area. The goalkeeper starts at the post.

Procedure

The goalkeeper performs two-foot lateral jumps over each of three hurdles. Keepers should clear the hurdles slightly, and after hitting the ground, drive-jump over the next one. After the goalkeeper clears the third hurdle, server 1 takes a shot. The goalkeeper saves the shot, sends the ball back, and returns to the post to start again. To train movement to the other side, place the cones on the opposite half of the goal and have the keeper begin from the other post.

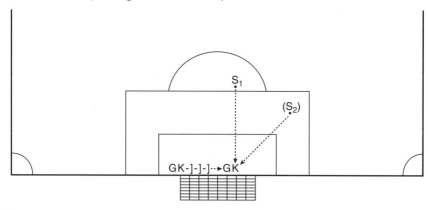

Repetitions

Perform four to six reps on each side.
Exercises in which keepers leap over obstacles should be used primarily in preseason, because if it's done correctly it takes a lot out of the keepers' legs and they need time to recover. During the season their legs should not become fatigued like that.

STRENGTH TRAINING

If coaches and keepers at the upper ages have the ability to get into a weight room and work with a strength coach, they should *do it*. Strength coaches can design a program that is geared for *soccer only*. If the strength coaches do not fully understand the demands of goalkeeping, the keeper and keeper coach can meet with the strength coach or invite him or her to a training session so they can see the movements that keepers need to perform. This will help them to design a program that is based on goalkeeping.

Weight training programs must be adapted to suit the age and aptitude of the individual keeper. Goalkeepers who don't have access to a strength training coach or experience in weight training should consult a professional.

I've been very fortunate to work with Jason Riley, one of the nation's top strength and conditioning coaches, who has trained such athletes as baseball stars Derek Jeter and Ryan Howard as well as scores of top-level soccer players, including national team and professional goalkeepers. He has trained keepers for Major League Soccer's Real Salt Lake and the U-17 and U-20 U.S. national teams. Riley recommends a strength training program for goalkeepers that includes the workouts shown in table 12.2.

Table 12.2 Sample Strength Training Session for Goalkeepers

Exercise	Weight and number of repetitions
Lower body	
Bulgarian squat	3 sets of 8-10: off-season 2 sets of 6-8: preseason 2 sets of 5: in-season
Dumbbell Romanian deadlift	3 sets of 8-10: off-season 2 sets of 6-8: preseason 2 sets of 5: in-season
Physioball single-leg curl	3 sets of 8-10: off-season 2 sets of 6-8: preseason 2 sets of 5: in-season
Upper body	
Dumbbell physioball bench press	3 sets of 10-12: off-season 2 sets of 6-8: preseason 2 sets of 4-6: in-season
Rotational pull-up	3 sets of 10-12: off-season 2 sets of 6-8: preseason 2 sets of 4-6: in-season
Dumbbell triceps pullover	3 sets of 10-12: off-season 2 sets of 6-8: preseason 2 sets of 4-6: in-season
Other	
Supine hip bridge	2 × 8-12 each
Off-bench front pillar	2 × 30-60 s
Draw-in single-leg lower*	2 × 8-12 each
Supine crunch roll-up	2 × 10-15
Bicycle crunch—extended	2 × 8-12 each
Back extension with twist	2 × 8-12 each
Front pillar with single-arm raise	2 × 8-12 each
Side pillar	2 × 30-60 s
Physioball prayer roll-out	2 × 10-15
Physioball supine hip bridge with leg raise	2 × 8-12 each
Physioball stabilization (hands on, circle)	2 × 10-15 each
Physioball stabilization (feet on, alternate leg raise)	2 × 8-12 each

Exercise	Weight and number of repetitions
Other *(continued)*	
Single-leg hip extension	2 × 12 each
Single-leg cable hip adduction	2 × 12 each
Single-leg hop to stabilization*	2 × 8-12 each
Shoulder combo 1	2 × 8-12 each
Standing scaption raise	2 × 8-10
Standing shoulder abduction	2 × 10-15 each
Bent-over T raise	2 × 5-8 each
Bent-over 90/90 external rotation	2 × 12 each
Scapular floor slide	1-3 min
Medicine ball rapid response* (chest, forehead, overhead)	
Prone V, T, Y raise	
Cable side external rotation	
Foam roll (iliotibial band, quads, tensor fasciae latae)	

Single-Leg Hop to Stabilization (Multiplanar)

Stand on right foot. Hop forward off right foot and land on right foot, focusing on landing position (hips back, chest forward, back flat, knee not past toes, and balanced on foot). The goal is to stick the landing with no extra movements. After sticking this movement, jump backward to the start position, focusing on the same mechanics. Jump to your right, stick landing, then jump back to start position. Jump at a 45-degree angle (between the first two points), stick landing, and hop back to start position. Repeat the same sequence at a 45-degree angle to the left and at a 90-degree angle from the start to the left (there are five points), then repeat on left leg.

Draw-In Single-Leg Lower

Lie on back with hips flexed at 90 degrees and both feet straight up in the air (L shape). Slowly lower both legs, making sure to draw in (pull navel toward spine, but breathe normally; don't hold breath). Lower legs only partially so that you can maintain the draw-in mechanics. The low back does not come off the floor or arch. Once you reach that position, that is the start position.

Slowly lower one leg toward the floor while maintaining the opposite leg in the extended position. Then slowly raise leg back up to start position and repeat on the other side, alternating legs, until you complete desired reps.

Medicine Ball Rapid Response

This exercise strengthens the rotator cuff and triceps and increases resistance to fatigue.

Overhead: Stand upright next to either a concrete wall or a squared-off goalpost. Position yourself so that you are only about 8 to 10 inches (25 cm) away from the wall. Extend arms overhead while holding a 2-kilogram or 3-kilogram medicine ball and dribble the ball against the wall overhead, keeping elbows in tight and as you catch the ball off the wall. Bend at the elbows so that the ball drops behind the head. The goal is to get as many touches against the wall in the specified time.

Forehead: Immediately after time is called, take one small step backward. Keep the ball at forehead level and dribble the ball against the wall again, but hands will be in front of shoulders rather than overhead.

Chest: Immediately after time is called, take one small step backward. Keep the ball at chest level with elbows in tight. Dribble the ball against the wall again, creating a little more power this time because the distance between you and the wall is not increased again.

Even the youngest keepers can use their own bodies to do strength training. They can do push-ups, pull-ups, squats using only body weight, and sit-ups. These body-weight exercises will help young keepers build strength without risking injury. Keepers can begin by doing a small number of repetitions, stopping when they begin to strain, and gradually increasing the number as they gain strength.

At the highest levels it is not possible to be successful without a year-round strength program. All three seasons (preseason, in-season, postseason) will require different approaches to weight training.

Preseason weight training prepares keepers for the demands of the coming season. During the season, the goals are maintenance of strength and injury prevention. Postseason is the time to strive to make the most progress in terms of strength gains. The off-season affords the keeper the luxury of focusing on specific areas in which she can improve physically. It's an opportunity not to be squandered, because during the season so much of a keeper's training time must be dedicated to gamelike situations.

SPEED AND AGILITY

Speed and agility are best trained outside of the goal. Tools such as speed ladders and agility rings (see figure 12.1) are excellent for developing speed and agility. Speed ladders are great for developing fast feet and change-of-direction skills. Rings and cones set up to work on cutting and change of direction are valuable as well. Have players move through the ladders or rings in a forward direction first, using one-foot hops out and then two-foot jumps back. Then have players move laterally through the ladders or cones, out in one direction and back in another.

When we try to force these tools into goalkeeping exercises, they don't make sense. It's not goalkeeping if it becomes gymnastics. Exercises that use rings and ladders are great to use as part of an extended warm-up before the keeper gets into goal. As a rule, keepers should focus on exercises that improve general speed and agility in the off-season. In preseason and in-season, goalkeepers must work to improve their sport-specific skills.

Figure 12.1 Agility ladder exercises challenge the keeper's foot-speed and coordination. The quicker and more automatic a keeper's footwork becomes, the freer he is to focus on other aspects of goalkeeping.

EYE–HAND COORDINATION AND QUICK REACTIONS

Goalkeepers need to have catlike reflexes to save balls hit from close range at great pace. They also need to have exceptional eye–hand coordination for catching. These skills can be honed through a variety of exercises. In addition to the drills that involve throwing assorted types and sizes of balls off a wall and having the keeper catch them (as noted in chapter 1), keepers can improve by playing other ball sports such as baseball, basketball, and volleyball.

Reflex Exercises

Tretiak Shuffle

Named after the legendary Russian ice hockey goalkeeper Vladislav Tretiak, this drill is excellent for eye–hand coordination. It can be performed alone and is part of rapid-response and reaction training.

Setup

Goalkeeper stands 4 feet (1.2 m) from a wall with a tennis ball in each hand.

Procedure

Using the right hand, the goalkeeper throws a tennis ball underhand at a wall and then moves slightly to the right and catches the rebound overhand in the right hand. The goalkeeper repeats the process with the left hand.

Repetitions

Perform 30- to 40-second bouts. Use 1:1 work-to-rest ratio.

Rapid Response in Goal

This exercise involves moving the feet quickly and developing eye–hand coordination while training reaction and reflexes.

Setup

Place two cones 4 to 6 yards off the goal line, 4 yards apart and centered on the goal. Server 1 has six tennis balls and stands a few yards in front of keeper, who begins between the two cones. Server 2 is positioned near the corner of the penalty area.

Procedure

Server 1 tosses a ball to the goalkeeper's right. The goalkeeper slaps the ball down and quickly moves to his left. Server 1 throws a ball to the goalkeeper's left and the goalkeeper slaps the ball down. After six slap-downs of the tennis balls (three to each side), server 2 sends the soccer ball toward the goal, and the goalkeeper saves the shot.

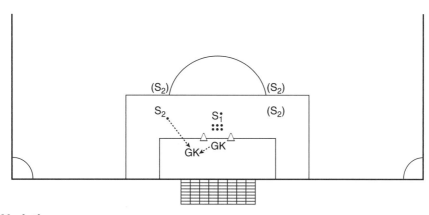

Variations

Goalkeeper catches tennis balls with one hand. Goalkeeper catches ball with two hands.

SEASONAL CONDITIONING

Good goalkeepers don't punch the clock or take long vacations. They take advantage of every opportunity to improve. What enables them to excel at game time is that they take advantage of opportunities to improve in the off-season, the preseason, and the in-season.

Preseason: Gradual Buildup

Preseason training is the time for the keeper to build on the work from the off-season (postseason) and prepare for the coming season. Preseason training should not begin with rigorous physical training because that can lead to injury. The training should gradually lead to very intense work. That intensity should build until it is time to taper off so that by no less than a week before the first game the keeper has hit the peak of fitness.

Starting out of the gate at warp speed will lead to injuries. Start off with moderate work efforts and build to peak intensity. By the time preseason has ended, a keeper should feel conditioned and fresh and confident for the season.

As the start of the season draws closer, training remains intense. But the aim is to maintain fitness rather than build it, and the focus is on skill and form. See the preseason section of table 12.3 on page 186 for a detailed example of a weekly preseason conditioning plan for high school athletes.

In-Season: Day by Day

This is where the goalkeeper coach earns the money. Much thought and planning should go into every training session. Treat each session as an opportunity to get better. Looking at it strictly from the physical standpoint, the aim should be maintenance and injury prevention. If a keeper comes out of preseason training healthy and fit, the goal is to maintain that state through the season. Review the training schedule weekly and monthly. Assess the number of games to be played, the number of training opportunities, and the travel schedule. Then design a program that facilitates a high level of play. See the in-season section of table 12.3 for a detailed example of a weekly in-season conditioning plan for high school athletes.

Here is a summary of a sample week of training for high-level players that is based around Saturday games:

Sunday. The day after the match should be a recovery day for the starter and a solid training session for the other keepers.

Monday. Resume training with a fairly light day of work at moderate intensity. Ball handling and footwork should be the basis of this training.

Tuesday. Push the limits a bit. Keep exercises going to the point where the player is noticeably fatigued and struggling a bit to keep good form. This is also a great day to address any problem areas observed in the previous match.

Wednesday. This is a day off.

Thursday. We come back and get after it at a quick tempo and with a strong effort. Early in the season the Tuesday and Thursday workouts can be pretty intense because the keepers are still fresh. As the season progresses, these should still be work days but the intensity might have to be reduced to help the keepers maintain their stamina and avoid injury. Always watch the keepers for signs of injuries and ask them how they feel.

Friday. This is a polish day. All routines should be short, sharp, and successful. A good competitive small-sided game to get the competitive juices flowing is always great on Fridays.

Saturday. Sit back and enjoy watching your keeper post a shutout.

Remember, you will have to push the second and third keepers harder to keep up their fitness levels. This can be built into every session by simply giving them extra work.

Game Day: Early Start

It is important for keepers, no matter what level they are at, to do something early in the day on match day. Their nervous system needs to be activated early on in the day so that when it's time for kickoff they are alert and ready to compete.

Staying in bed and resting only make players lethargic and lazy. Most professional teams play at night, so some light work is done early in the day to prime the nervous system. Speed ladder work followed by stretching is a good example. These sessions should last 40 minutes total for adult keepers and include hopping and jumping movements as well as running in forward and lateral directions.

If the game is in the afternoon, a brisk 20- to 30-minute walk and some light stretching after breakfast are perfect. Backup keepers should work out in the same manner as the starter so they are on the same schedule and ready to play if called on.

Postseason: Time to Improve

There's a saying that *players* get better in the off-season and *teams* get better during the season. How true. The focus of the postseason should be on improving all the physical, technical, and tactical deficiencies of the individual players so that they are at their best and ready to band together as a unit when they come together again.

Coaches should devise or recommend a strength and conditioning program to build on their keepers' level of conditioning from the previous season. During the postseason, players can devote as much time as necessary to physical development. Keepers who don't have goalkeeper coaches can work with their regular coaches, perhaps in consultation with a keeper coach and strength coach, to devise a program. See the off-season section of table 12.3 for a detailed example of a weekly postseason conditioning plan for high school athletes.

Strength and conditioning expert Jason Riley, who helped design conditioning programs for the U.S. soccer youth national team, recommends the program presented in table 12.3 for goalkeepers who have reached their mid-teens.

Table 12.3 Sample Annual Conditioning Program*

Off-season		
Day	**Exercise or activity**	**Repetitions or duration**
Sunday	Off	
Monday	Weight room—lower body	60 min 8-10 reps
Tuesday	Weight room—upper body Agility and movement	90 min, 10-12 reps 30 min
Wednesday	Light conditioning Recovery (pool, contrast bath, mobility)	20-30 min 15-20 min
Thursday	Weight room—total body	60 min
Friday	Agility Conditioning—hard	45 min 20-25 min
Saturday	Recovery (pool, contrast bath, mobility)	20 min
Preseason		
Day	**Exercise or activity**	**Repetitions or duration**
Sunday	Off	
Monday	Weight room—total body	45-60 min, 6-8 reps
Tuesday	Agility and conditioning	45-60 min
Wednesday	Recovery	30 min
Thursday	Weight room	45-60 min, 6-8 reps
Friday	Agility and conditioning	45-60 min
Saturday	Recovery	
In-season		
Day	**Exercise or activity**	**Repetitions or duration**
Sunday	Off	
Monday	Weight room—total body	5-6 reps lower, 4-6 reps upper
Tuesday	Mobility and agility	30 min
Wednesday	Recovery	30 min
Thursday	Weight room—total body	5-6 reps lower, 4-6 reps upper
Friday	Mobility and agility	30 min
Saturday	Off	

*For goalkeepers 14 and older.

However, the technical and tactical development of the keeper should not be neglected. Players usually have no problem getting in the weight room and pumping iron in the off-season. They are willing to try all the latest exercises in an effort to become more powerful, faster, and stronger. The tougher job for the coach may be to get the athletes to work on the other areas of their game. Besides designing an off-season fitness program, the coach needs to work with the keeper to design an off-season technical program and tactical program.

Assess the keepers' play and create a program that will work on their weaknesses and build on their strengths. At the higher levels, the keeper coaches should be available to work with their keepers anywhere from four to six days a week. The sessions need to be based on technical improvements.

On the tactical front, coaches should assess how many of their keepers study film. Encourage keepers to watch all of the previous season's games to assess strengths and weaknesses. Help them to obtain and study video of the best keepers in the league. Put together a tape or DVD of actions by the team's keepers that are particularly worthy of study. Give them to the keepers and ask that they view them. Getting together to view and discuss them during the off-season is an even better idea. As the legendary UCLA basketball coach John Wooden used to say, echoing Benjamin Franklin, "Failing to prepare is preparing to fail."

CIRCUIT TRAINING

Circuit training is a great way to combine conditioning with goalkeeping activities. It works well during the season when outdoor training is not an option or as a change of pace. A coach can set up several stations and have the keeper work for 40 to 60 seconds at each station. The keeper gets 30 to 45 seconds for a break between circuits and then starts the next exercise. These stations can be anything that involves goalkeeping and conditioning. The goal is to make the keeper work through a variety of exercises. These sessions should last an hour.

Here is an example of a circuit provided by Coach Riley:

Circuit Drills*

Lateral Microhurdle Shuffle

This drill develops fast feet. Place two hurdles about 2 feet (60 cm) apart. Facing sideways, keep both feet outside the first hurdle. When the coach says go, laterally run through the hurdles (two feet will be in middle of hurdles, but only one foot will ever be outside hurdles). Keep this movement continuous until the coach says stop.

Medicine Ball Crunch to Throw

This drill creates strength on the lowering phase and power on the throwing phase. Sit on the ground and bend your knees so your feet are flat to the ground. A partner stands about 4 to 5 yards away and tosses a ball over your head. Catch the ball and slowly descend, resisting the weight of the ball pulling you down to the ground. Once your entire back touches the ground, use your abdominal muscles to sit up, and throw the ball back to your partner as fast as you can. Do not let the arms do all the work.

(continued)

---

*For goalkeepers 14 and older.

Fast-Feet Box Drill

This drill develops fast feet. Stand in front of a box that is about 2 to 6 inches (10 cm) in height. Place the left foot on the box and the right foot on the ground in front of the box; weight will be mostly on the right leg. On the go signal, continuously switch your feet between the ground and the box. Do as many reps as possible in the allotted time.

Line Skier

This drill develops change of direction skills and balance. Place both feet on the right side of a line on the field. On the go signal, quickly hop side to side over the line so that both feet simultaneously contact the ground. Stay in an athletic stance with hips, knees, and ankles slightly flexed and weight on the balls of the feet. The upper body should lean slightly forward so that you are always in a balanced position.

Medicine Ball Overhead Chop

This drill creates power through the core. Stand with the feet shoulder-width apart and a 3- to 4-kilogram medicine ball in your hands. Slowly bring the ball overhead. Extend through hips, knees, and ankles and then chop the ball toward the ground about 2 to 3 feet (.8 m) in front of your toes. The ending position should be with your hips slightly flexed and your torso leaning forward.

Weave Drill Forward and Backward

This drill develops footwork and coordination. Place seven cones in two lines in a staggered formation; the two lines should be about 3 yards apart. Staying in a defensive position, weave your way forward through the cones. Once you reach the last cone, continue weaving through the cones backward. When going backward, work on opening the hips and moving as quickly as possible. Repeat for the allotted time.

Circle Run With Change of Direction

This drill develops core strength and balance and change of direction skills. Place cones in a circle about 5 to 7 yards in diameter. (The smaller the circle, the harder the drill.) Start in an athletic stance and sprint around a circle as fast as you can, facing forward and leaning into the middle of the circle slightly so inertia doesn't pull you away from the cones. Focus on maintaining a tight core and allowing the force to be applied through the inside and outside edges of the feet. Once you get to the starting point, stop your momentum, change direction (facing the circle), and sprint in the opposite direction around the circle.

Single-Leg T-Balance Rotation

This drill creates ankle, knee, and hip stability and trains the posterior tibialis muscles, which help maintain the arch in your foot, allowing for more efficient movement patterns and decreasing the risk of injury. Standing on the right leg, bend to a 90-degree angle at the waist and extend both arms to the side (like a plane) as you extend the left leg straight behind you, trying to make a T shape with your body. Once balanced, slowly rotate your shoulders toward your right leg and then away from your right leg.

Medicine Ball Lunge Throw

This drill develops dynamic core strength and hip stability. A partner stands about 5 yards away and to your right. Lunge forward with the left leg forward so that the ankle and knee are aligned (the knee is not past the toes). Keep the right leg straight by squeezing the glutes. Have a partner throw the medicine ball to you so that the ball passes over the left knee. Catch the ball, decelerating it. Keep the arms extended and throw the ball back to your partner as hard as you can without losing balance and without letting the knee or hip move.

Icky Shuffle Ladder Drill

This drill develops coordination and foot skills. Using an agility ladder, perform the drill depicted in the following diagram. Stepping on one foot at a time, travel forward down the ladder and then backward as fast as possible until time is called: right 1 outside the ladder, left 2 inside, right 3 inside, left 4 outside, and so on.

L 4		L 10	
L2	L6	L8	L12
R3	R5	R9	R11

R 1   R 7   R 13

Medicine Ball Overhead Rapid-Response Drill

This drill increases endurance through the rotator cuff and triceps. Grab a 2- or 3-kilogram medicine ball and stand about 8 inches (20 cm) in front of a concrete wall or squared-off goalpost. Take the ball overhead. As quickly as you can, dribble the ball between the wall and your hands with the arms extended overhead, bending only at the elbows. Maintain a tight core by drawing the navel in and maintaining a good athletic stance. Once time is called, immediately take one small step away from the wall and do the same drill with the arms extended in front at about forehead height. Do the same thing one more time at chest level.

Resisted Lateral Shuffle

This drill develops power and strength and works on lateral movement. Set up two cones 5 yards apart. Loop an exercise band around your waist while a partner standing beside one of the cones holds onto the ends of the band. Stand in athletic stance. Without letting the feet come closer than shoulder-width apart, shuffle sideways between the cones and then back to the start position. Repeat as many times as possible in the allotted time while maintaining balance.

Index

Note: The italicized *t* and *f* following page numbers refer to tables and figures, respectively.

About the Authors

Tim Mulqueen has been coaching goalkeepers at all levels since 1990 and is currently the goalkeeper coach with the United States national teams. He is also the goalkeeper instructor for the U.S. Soccer Federation A, B, and C licenses and has helped in the establishment and curriculum for the newly formed U.S. Soccer Federation goalkeeping license.

Mulqueen was an assistant coach and goalkeeper coach for the United States at the 2008 Olympic Games in Beijing. He has coached athletes who have gone on to achieve worldwide recognition, including England Premier League players Tim Howard, Kasey Keller, Marcus Hahnemann, and Brad Guzan. Before joining U.S. Soccer, Mulqueen coached in the MLS where he won the 2000 MLS Cup and Supporters Shield. While in the MLS, Tim coached Zach Thornton, who went on to win the 1998 Goalkeeper of the Year award. Tim also coached U.S. international goalkeeper Tony Meola when, in 2000, he became the only goalkeeper to win the MLS MVP Award, in addition to being named Goalkeeper of the Year. Mulqueen has coached in four Youth World Cups, two at the U-20 level and two at the U-17 level. He resides in Bradenton, Florida, with his wife, Kathleen, his son, Trevor, and daughter, Cate.

Photo by Tony Quinn

Mike Woitalla is the executive editor of *Soccer America*, where he has worked since 1985. He has covered four World Cups for the magazine and has reported on soccer from 17 nations. His freelance articles have appeared in more than 30 media outlets in eight countries.

Woitalla is a regular contributor to the British soccer monthly *When Saturday Comes* and has won six NSCAA Writing Contest awards as well as two Professional Soccer Reporters of America awards. He is the coauthor of former U.S. national team captain Claudio Reyna's book *More Than Goals*.

Woitalla is a graduate of the University of California at Berkeley, where he was a member of the Golden Bears varsity soccer team. He currently coaches youth soccer and is married to Holly Kernan, a public radio producer, host, and reporter. They live in Oakland, California, with their daughter, Julia.

CONTENTS